now and not yet

Other Books by
RUTH CHOU SIMONS

———

GraceLaced

Beholding and Becoming

Foundations

TruthFilled

When Strivings Cease

When Strivings Cease Bible Study

Emmanuel

Pilgrim

now and not yet

PRESSING IN WHEN YOU'RE WAITING, WANTING, AND RESTLESS FOR MORE

RUTH CHOU SIMONS

NELSON
BOOKS

An Imprint of Thomas Nelson

Published in Nashville, Tennessee, by Thomas Nelson. Thomas Nelson is a registered trademark of HarperCollins Christian Publishing, Inc.

Published in association with William K. Jensen Literary Agency, 119 Bampton Court, Eugene, Oregon 97404.

Thomas Nelson titles may be purchased in bulk for educational, business, fundraising, or sales promotional use. For information, please email SpecialMarkets@ThomasNelson.com.

ISBN 978-1-4002-4832-2 (ITPE)

Library of Congress Cataloging-in-Publication Data

Names: Chou Simons, Ruth, author.
Title: Now and not yet: pressing in when you're waiting, wanting, and restless for more / Ruth Chou Simons.
Description: Nashville: Thomas Nelson, [2023] | Includes bibliographical references. | Summary: "Bestselling author Ruth Chou Simons guides readers who are restless in their current circumstances on a journey of growth, purpose, and pressing in"-- Provided by publisher.
Identifiers: LCCN 2023044019 (print) | LCCN 2023044020 (ebook) | ISBN 9781400225057 (hardcover) | ISBN 9781400225064 (epub)
Subjects: LCSH: Christian life. | Perseverance (Ethics) | Diligence.
Classification: LCC BV4501.3 .C485 2023 (print) | LCC BV4501.3 (ebook) | DDC 248.4--dc23/ eng20231205
LC record available at https://lccn.loc.gov/2023044019
LC ebook record available at https://lccn.loc.gov/2023044020

Printed in the United States of America

24 25 26 27 28 LBC 5 4 3 2 1

To Troy, my closest friend for the last twenty-five years of this now-and-not-yet life. You've taught me how to steward the right now in light of eternity more than you'll ever know simply by the way you live, love, and refuse to give up.

Contents

Contents

Introduction

The Good Life always seems to be running ahead of me. She's just around the corner, where I lose sight of her while tripping on the shoelaces I have to slow down to tie. Sometimes I imagine her high-fiving the smart, savvy, put-together over-achievers in the corner office as they accomplish yet another goal while I'm waiting in the carpool lane. Other times I look up from my endless sink-full of dishes long enough to see the Good Life stroll by, arm in arm with carefree friends, laughing and sipping mocha lattes, and I sigh.

I want to be *there*, not here.

And what exactly do I imagine the Good Life to be? She's unburdened, joyful, confident, and free. She's moved past her pain, troubles, and obstacles. She's purposeful, skilled, and using her gifts exactly the way she hopes. And, perhaps most of all, she feels unhurried and at home exactly where she is—today, right now, in this very moment.

Every day, I think I'll finally catch up with the Good Life, only to find she's eluded me yet again.

Introduction

If you've picked up this book, my assumption is that your right now—your life circumstances, relationships, inner dialogues, intimacy with God, progress, daily grind, challenges, or how your best-laid plans have turned out—is not everything you hoped for. Sure, you may be sitting at your favorite coffee shop at the moment, or rocking your sleeping baby on your front porch, or enjoying a quiet afternoon as you begin this book, and this exact moment may feel rather sweet to savor. *Thank God. What grace.* But soon, the moment of ease passes, the reprieve ends, and the reality of life's persistent pressures, disappointments, heartaches, unresolved issues, detours, and all that's not yet wonderful comes flooding into your mind again. You don't know if you're allowed to say it, let alone think it, but you just don't want to be here right now.

I understand that more than you know. I'm with you, friend. And I'm committed to honesty, so I'll just go ahead and say it: *right now is hard; I'd rather skip it altogether.*

Yesterday might be revealing, *someday* may be promising, but *right now . . . right now* can seem so far from where we really long to be.

And where we'd rather be is somewhere where we're . . .

- beyond (the challenge, the pain, the trial),
- seen and known by others,
- not a hot mess,
- doing what we think we're meant for,
- grace-laced and faith-filled,
- joyful in our circumstances,

Yesterday
might be
revealing,
Someday may be
promising, but
right now...
right now can seem
so far from where
we really
long to be.

- working with a shorter prayer request list,
- flourishing,
- on the other side of the life lessons we don't want to learn,
- amid opportunities that display our strengths (not our weaknesses),
- no longer grieving,
- encircled by community, and
- visibly making an impact.

This list is straight from my own journal. I'd rather be there too.

But I'm not there . . . *not yet*. And, likely, neither are you, whatever your "there" is. Both of us are in the middle of right here, right now—with all the life circumstances and heart situations we've been given to work with. The tension created by the gap between what we want our circumstances to be and how they really are is real. And sometimes we struggle to see the point of all we must endure in this current season. I know I do.

I look around and see abundant resources for processing the past and unending resources for achieving the future we might envision for ourselves. But what about right now—the right now we honestly don't quite know how to rejoice in, persist in, thrive in?

Do we need to toughen up and grind it out? Are we supposed to numb ourselves with distractions from our disappointments? Do we trust in ourselves and buy into a system of belief that tells us we can control our own lives?

Or is there a better way?

Introduction

You may be thinking, *Okay, Ruth, are you going to teach me how to create the life I really want? Can you share the secret to being magically grateful for my current realities?* Friend, you don't know how many times I've wished for an Easy button to navigate my unexpected, unwanted, and not-according-to-plan circumstances. I wish our self-made formulas worked for the deepest longings of our lives, but they don't. Solutions that treat only the symptoms will never fully heal the pain.

But I do want to offer you something much greater than my best strategy for creating the life you want or a mind game that causes you to have a positive attitude about everything. There really is a better way.

I want to lead you to something more powerful: the truth about what God says about our unwanted and not-yet-wonderful circumstances and how he works in and through them, even now.

If we were having coffee (yep, if you know me, you know how much I'd rather share all these things during a coffee date), I'd tell you . . .

It's okay not to like the right now you've been given.

You don't have to like it to lean into it.

Your right now really matters.

I've learned again and again, in season after season, that God is purposeful about what happens between today and tomorrow, between right now and someday. And I truly believe your current season is not wasted.

The journey we're entering together is an honest one. It will require facing the unwanted realities of right now and choosing to press in and not check out. It means actively engaging with

xiii

things that don't come naturally to us, rejoicing when it's hard, and preparing for what we can't even imagine is possible from our current vantage point.

This book is for those of us who are waiting, wanting, and restless for more.

And my prayer is that we stop hiding behind simple platitudes and quick fixes to our unwanted right nows and bravely step into the ways God wants to change us . . . instead of staying busy trying to change our circumstances.

We can press into all the not yets of our daily lives instead of just surviving our circumstances until they align with our expectations.

We can know God is at work right now when we don't see the progress we're looking for.

We can stop waiting for someday to arrive and take the next step with what we've already been given.

Your someday begins today.

We can flip the script on the story we're telling ourselves about our current circumstances when we can't yet see all the chapters of our lives.

Friend, your someday begins today. So start where you are right now . . . because this moment matters.

Chapter 1

When Right Now Isn't What You Want

Twenty-one years ago my husband, Troy, and I welcomed our first son into the world. Two years later, I gave birth to another boy. And again two years later, and again two years after that. A fifth boy joined our family another two years later, and a final son was born eleven years after we began our parenting journey. If you were counting, you're not mistaken—that's six sons in just over a decade. We were overjoyed and more than a little exhausted.

During that season, Troy was a pastor of a church plant as well as the headmaster of a school we helped found. We also moved into and remodeled three homes, started a website, and then started a business, all within the same decade. (For the record, I do *not* recommend this.) We were optimistic, ambitious, and full of energy. We had so much vision for what was yet to come: a finished home, a healthy church, an established school, easier days ahead in marriage and parenting, fulfilling and purposeful use of our giftings, and more time, money, and resources. Someday.

So imagine my disappointment when motherhood didn't come naturally to me but instead kept revealing more and more of my impatience, selfishness, and lack of self-control.

Or when marriage felt impossibly difficult.

Or when I felt capsized by ministry hurt while trying to keep my head above water.

Or when my college education seemed to be wasted on sweeping up Cheerios.

Or when *someday when I have more time* never came, and my lack of consistency with God and in reading his Word began to leave me feeling empty, distant, and ashamed.

Or when messy family relationships and friendships didn't resolve neatly, and I had no choice but to pursue what I could when other paths to peace were not available.

Imagine waking up to a reality that isn't all that you hoped it would be.

My guess is that you don't have to imagine; you know exactly what I'm talking about.

Even if our life seasons and stories aren't the same, we all know what it is to long for what is not yet ours. We know how it feels to want something other than what we have right in front of us. I don't know about you, but I am often so ready to be on the other side of my right-now circumstances and fully thriving in what I think is so much more, so much better, that I can't yet see or taste in the now.

People say gratitude turns what you have into enough, but

isn't living out that paradigm such a mystery? How can you be happy in your *right now* when your *not yet* feels so far away?

I hope you're reading this vulnerable confession and nodding in agreement. Of course, I don't wish for you to be angsty or uncomfortable in your current situation; I just hope that you, dear reader, understand what it feels like to wrestle with today. To feel so done with your right now.

The Parts We'd Rather Skip

"I'm so done with this," I complained. It was maybe 2010. I was so deep in the little years I could barely keep track of birthdays. I just knew that I had a whole bunch of littles, likely under eight years of age. These words—most often kept in my journal—I muttered aloud that day to Troy after one of our six young sons accidentally dropped a Costco-sized jar of bread-and-butter pickles on the tile floor.

The pickles had been added to the cart as a treat, a nonessential on a tight grocery budget. They were just pickles, but for me (a young mom who had successfully made it home from a tiring trip to the store), tears of defeat were the natural response in the moment. A kaleidoscope of shattered glass radiated across the kitchen floor, and a river of sticky, sweet brine slithered and pooled under the kitchen island while the baby splashed in a puddle and another mancub stepped into the syrupy mess and tracked size-one footprints throughout the house before anyone noticed and snatched him up.

It wasn't a tragedy; it was an accident we could laugh about later. But for an exhausted mom who, in her quiet moments, couldn't make sense of why God would give her six little boys in the first place (when she had pictured herself with a tidy and seemingly manageable one-boy-and-one-girl combo), this pickle jar debacle added to a long list of *not what I wanteds, not what I hoped fors,* and *more than I can endures.*

"Come on, really?" I protested. *Is this necessary, God? Do I really need to be here right now? Can we skip to the good part?*

If any of the work-in-progress areas of my life in that season—parenting, ministry, marriage, friendships—had been packaged as Home Depot growing kits, the instructions would've appropriately said, "Just add tireless work and lots of time." And the warning label would have read, in tiny print,

> *Warning:* May result in conflict, heartache, suffering, and loss of friendships. May experience purposelessness, discontent, chaos, and overwhelm. Results may vary. Serious cases of weakness and inadequacy have occurred.

We didn't have much in savings, rarely slept through the night uninterrupted, and hardly had time to refuel before feeling completely drained again the next day.

For all that we lacked, we did have a robust portfolio of endeavors we had started with an end in mind. With a vision for someday. But now—in the midst of all the realities between what was and what could be—was not what I had imagined, and it certainly was not what I wanted in the moment.

I wanted to hit Next on the control panel of my life. I had prayed for some of these very opportunities. I wanted what God had given me; I just didn't want a version that included unknowns, unrewarded attempts at the right choice, unending obstacles, struggles with my own weaknesses, and a restless lack of fulfillment. I didn't want to feel those feelings, and I didn't know what to do with those feelings. Sometimes I prayed about it. Sometimes I talked to Troy and trusted friends. Sometimes I scrolled Facebook for too many hours. Sometimes I put a smile on my face and muscled my way through the day.

It's hard to live on purpose in the present when your expectations take you somewhere else.

All I could think was, *If only I knew what God was doing in my present reality, perhaps then I could really enjoy where I'm at because I'd know how my story will make sense in the end.*

———

This might be a good time for me to confess something I'm not proud of: I'm an impatient movie watcher. I've been known to hit the Forward-Fifteen-Seconds button on streaming platforms to get to the parts I really care about while skipping all I deem unnecessary. *I get the idea. No need for another montage.* I want to know what happens next. And I don't do well with suspenseful plot twists. Of course, I enjoy all the twists and turns after the credits roll. *Wow, that was unexpected! I didn't see that coming, but that was the best part! Oh, now I wanna see it again!* But in the moment? In the moment, I just want to take a bathroom break, even if I don't really need it.

Sometimes I do step out of the room when watching a movie because it's just too much for me to handle. And other times, I've been known to Google the plotline while the movie is playing, to read ahead on what happens next so I can stop feeling anxious about what I'm experiencing in the moment. I

It's hard to live on purpose in the present when your expectations take you somewhere else.

know. It's annoying to watch movies with me. I'm sorry. You may not believe me, but sometimes I end up enjoying the movie more after I've read the plot summary, when I can settle in, knowing where the film is heading rather than holding my breath while waiting for the stressful scene to be over. My boys can't believe I do this either.

But when I look to the Bible, God's Word written to us and for us, I see example after example of how God intentionally led his people through their impossible current circumstances rather than providing a shortcut around them. Perhaps the most poignant picture of this is in Exodus 14.

God had led the Israelites out of slavery in Egypt, which was a grand display of his power and care. But then Pharaoh changed his mind about letting his slave force go and sent his army after the Israelites. God's people were stopped at the Red Sea while the Egyptians were gaining on them. The end of their flight from captivity seemed imminent—until God instructed Moses to trust him with the way through:

> The LORD drove the sea back by a strong east wind all night and made the sea dry land, and the waters were divided. And the people of Israel went into the midst of the sea on dry ground, the waters being a wall to them on their right hand and on their left. (vv. 21–22)

God, in his power, could've easily diverted the enemy, slowed them down, or given the Israelites a way around the impossible obstacle, but instead, he chose to take them through it. He intentionally allowed his people to face an overwhelming circumstance and cry out to him. Why? Because the God of the universe wanted to make a way through for his people. He wanted to put his purpose on display. He wanted to show them that he provides a way where there seems to be no way:

> This is what the LORD says—
>> he who made a way through the sea,
>> a path through the mighty waters,
> who drew out the chariots and horses,
>> the army and reinforcements together,
> and they lay there, never to rise again,
>> extinguished, snuffed out like a wick:
> "Forget the former things;
>> do not dwell on the past.
> See, I am doing a new thing!
>> Now it springs up; do you not perceive it?
> I am making a way in the wilderness
>> and streams in the wasteland." (Isaiah 43:16–19 NIV)

The Israelites knew well this story of God's rescue. And we, living on the other side of the cross of Christ, know that God ultimately fulfilled his promise to redeem forever all who believe in Christ from the bondage and oppression of sin and death. God made a way through Jesus, "the way, and the truth, and the life" (John 14:6), the only way back to the presence of the Father. He made a way so that we could have true rest from chasing after all we think we must do or have in order to be satisfied.

Friend, even if you don't ruin movies like I do, you probably wrestle with wanting to know the plotline of your own story. Maybe you've hit what feels like an impossible point in your story, and you're so ready for what's next. You'd love to skip to the good part, the part where you're not holding your breath, the happy ending you long for. Perhaps, like me, you tend to look for a way out rather than a way through.

But the truth is, we don't get a Next or Fast-Forward button for life, and there is no Wikipedia page with a summary of how our current circumstances are momentum for the next part of the story.

It might feel like an unnecessary question, but I have to put it out there: If we are grateful people, and especially if we love the God who gave us life, why isn't it easier for us to enjoy each day, moment by moment, with all its unanswered questions, not-yet-fulfilled dreams, and bumps in the road? Why are we so tempted to skip the present and put our hope in what's next? Shouldn't we be happy and content if we are blessed in some way (and, in truth, we all are, regardless of circumstance)? Doesn't the Bible tell us, "This is the day that the LORD has made; let us rejoice and be glad in it" (Psalm 118:24)? Why do Christ followers struggle with waiting, wanting, and restlessness amid the messy middle of our lives?

I think it has something to do with our assumptions about God's character, our limited understanding of his ways, and the choices we get to make each day about how to realign and respond to what God says about his purposes, right where we are. When I look at the lives of men and women in the Bible— people God brought into his story of redemption—I see many examples of this very kind of wrestling to embrace and use what we've been given when we can't see how it'll all play out. You and I aren't the first ones to struggle to figure out how to be faithful and fruitful between here and there, the seen and unseen, hungry and satisfied, the now and not yet.

God is indeed purposeful right here, in the midst of it all. Because I've wrestled with these very thoughts in each season of my life, I truly believe that how we embrace our right now is a perennial and continual realigning of the heart. (Spoiler alert: *realigning* is to return to our God-intended perspective, posture, and purpose as image-bearers—more on this later in the book!) It doesn't happen by default, and it sure isn't easy, but I've discovered again and again that God is at work more than we yet know.

> How we embrace our right now is a perennial and continual realigning of the heart.

Sticky pickle juice and toddler footprints aren't my current season, and they may not be yours, but the truth is, even though the stream of unwanted circumstances looks and feels different from one season to the next, it is ever-present in the right nows of our lives. There's always something we'd rather skip, a circumstance we'd like to hit Next on. From where I'm writing these words to you, I'm a good decade out from the pickle-jar season, but every right now in my adult life has had equally challenging (albeit different) circumstances I'd rather skip altogether. The heart struggle is the same.

I invite you to take a minute here to pause. Perhaps you've already identified what your current sticky situation is. If not, these questions might help:

1. What unwanted or impossible reality in your right now seems unnecessary and purposeless for getting you to the someday you long for?

2. Where do you feel stuck in your current season?

This is not a one-and-done lesson in my life, and I'm assuming it won't be for you either. You have a choice to stay present, to not check out, to press into the unwanted parts of your story that are happening right now even if they don't feel purposeful or productive. The most life-transforming practices are ones that take time. They change your mind before they change your course.

Missionary and author Elisabeth Elliot wisely said, "The secret is Christ in *me*, not me in a different set of circumstances."[1] God is the God of the way through . . . through himself.

What does "Christ in me" mean for our next step in the midst of our disappointments, dreams deferred, and waiting for change? If our right believing leads to right living (which I believe it does), then we must bridge the distance between what we know in our heads and how we engage in our every day. We must replace our checked-out surviving with a framework for living in the now . . . when it's not yet.

We'll find this and more on our journey, friend. You're right where you need to be. Turn the page, but don't skip a thing.

TRUTH TO PRESS INTO

Even if today isn't what I want, God knows what I need.

A LITURGY FOR WHEN
EXPECTATIONS ARE UNMET

I have expectations, Lord, buried so deep inside me
that most friends and family will never fully know—
until my expectations erupt, boil over, and spread
to reveal my secret longings.
I am neither the master nor the ruler of my life,
so teach me to acknowledge what is true
and submit to
your rule and reign,
your wise ways,
your timing in all things,
your purpose in pain,
your allowance for disappointments,
your delay in deliverance.
Right now may not be what I want,
but tune my heart to sing your grace.
Even here, where I feel the dissonance
of being out of tune,
let me lean in and listen to the melody
of your faithfulness today,
so that even my expectations are transformed
into longings that reflect your heart for me.
Do what feels impossible for me
but is more than feasible by your hand, O Lord.
Amen.

Chapter 2

Restlessness as an Invitation

I recently saw an old photograph of me from college. My hair was short—a pixie cut, they called it. I knew that look by another name. It was the I'm-so-frustrated-I-don't-know-what-to-do-so-I'll-chop-off-all-my-hair hairdo. If I remember correctly, it was triggered by a tumultuous breakup with Troy before we got back together again. He really liked my long hair. I really wanted him to regret the pain he allegedly caused me. In retrospect, the drastic haircut wasn't purely to spite him; it was a desperate attempt to make some kind of change, any change, that might soothe my heart that had just been broken, that was restlessly looking for something. I felt impatient for change. I wanted to know where I was going in life and who I was going with. I was restless for more, and at the time, Troy just didn't have more to offer me.

It felt good in the moment to stare at a new me in the mirror. Instant change can be a thrill. But the excitement of chopping off all my hair was short-lived, and I soon found myself feeling unsettled again, as if something was missing. Unfortunately, that idea cost me many years of bad hairstyles. I learned the hard way that there are less extreme ways to deal with restlessness.

We're restless people. Even when our lives are full, we feel as if we're missing something, and we go searching for more.

The familiar refrain came up again the other day in a conversation with a friend: "I feel so restless." I've lost count of how many times this admission has surfaced among friends at small groups and dinner parties in recent months. I know what they mean because I've been there many times myself. And after so many years, I've come to hear the questions behind the statements:

Is this all there is?

How do I break out of my tedious life?

What if I want more?

What if I don't feel fulfilled?

How do I get where I want to go?

Is it okay to feel discontent?

Why am I unmotivated to press in right where I am?

What if I'm not passionate about the life I currently have?

Who am I, really?

What's my purpose in this one life I have?

If *restlessness* is defined as "the state of being unable to stay still or be happy where you are, because you are bored or need a change,"[1] then what I'm looking for when I'm feeling restless is relief from that unease. Here's the thing: I really want to be able to be still. Not just physically still—though actual sleep, rest, and the ability to stop working as if our whole lives depended on our efforts is absolutely necessary—but also mentally, emotionally, and spiritually still. I want to experience relief from anxious striving, worry, and the fear that the Good Life will pass me by. In a word, I'm after *peace*. When my heart is pacing the floor, I'm really looking for a way to rest.

What's at the heart of our longings for change, for something different, for something more? What's the real root cause of feeling stuck, as if what we have isn't enough?

When I peel back the layers of my restlessness, I always find, at the core, a fear that God doesn't know best, that somehow he didn't get the memo about what I really need, what I really want, or how my life should really turn out. I question where I am and what I've been given to work with. The core belief of restlessness stems from thinking I can't truly rest until I secure everything I think I need. It's safe to say my restlessness most often coincides with forgetfulness about where true rest comes from.

Restlessness Versus True Rest

The first book of the Bible reveals how we all became restless in the first place. You may remember the story: Adam and Eve had everything they could possibly desire, and, more importantly, they lived in the very presence of God. They had

My restlessness
most often coincides
with forgetfulness
about where true
rest comes from.

unhindered fellowship with their Creator, and all of creation was at rest. They didn't know a day apart from his care, and the Bible tells us that they existed as God created them—they were "naked and felt no shame" (Genesis 2:25). God gave them access to everything except for the fruit of the Tree of Knowledge of Good and Evil.

When the Serpent came to tempt Eve, he didn't tempt her with the fruit itself; he planted a question in her mind about what the fruit could give her access to. He questioned God's goodness and plan for Adam and Eve, and she took the bait. It's a familiar story, but I want us to read it anew and look for what Eve ultimately treasured in this biblical account:

> Now the serpent was more crafty than any of the wild animals the LORD God had made. He said to the woman, "Did God really say, 'You must not eat from any tree in the garden'?"
>
> The woman said to the serpent, "We may eat fruit from the trees in the garden, but God did say, 'You must not eat fruit from the tree that is in the middle of the garden, and you must not touch it, or you will die.'"
>
> "You will not certainly die," the serpent said to the woman. "For God knows that when you eat from it your eyes will be opened, and you will be like God, knowing good and evil."
>
> When the woman saw that the fruit of the tree was good for food and pleasing to the eye, and also desirable for gaining wisdom, she took some and ate it. She also gave some to her husband, who was with her, and he ate it. Then the eyes of both of them were opened, and they realized

they were naked; so they sewed fig leaves together and made coverings for themselves. (3:1–7 NIV)

Desirable for gaining wisdom. What did Eve ultimately treasure? She wanted to be like God, to know what he knows, to attain for herself what she didn't fully trust God to provide. You see, Eve's decision wasn't a momentary lapse in judgment, and she wasn't hypnotized by a shiny Red Delicious apple. Instead, she let herself believe that God was holding out on her, that he wasn't yet giving his best to her. So she opted to reach out and get it for herself. She wanted more. More than what God had provided. More than what he'd promised. More than God himself.

The unbelieving world often celebrates Eve's actions as powerful and assertive, but, friend, let's be clear: God gave Eve everything she would ever truly need to be the best version of who he made her to be. She lacked nothing. Eve was made to be fully satisfied in her creator God, and access to him without shame or obstacle was the greatest supernatural power she could ever experience. She gained nothing better by trusting in herself. She was looking for more than God's provision, but instead of giving her more, her search led to a restless longing within her and within every person since.

Because of sin, Adam and Eve knew shame for the first time and experienced a feeling they had not known prior: a sense of *not enough.*

Without the brokenness of sin, we wouldn't wrestle with waiting, wanting, and restlessness. Before Adam and Eve ate the fruit, feelings of not enough weren't a factor because God was fully and completely satisfying. Understand me clearly: it's not sinful to struggle with those feelings. The feelings themselves aren't sinful, but the temptation to find more on our own can lead to sinful responses if we try to substitute true rest in God with comfort in anything else.

Though sin, disbelief, discontent, and disobedience entered the world through Adam and Eve in the garden, God's plan has always been to restore us to the relationship we were intended for and the rest we were created for. Our restlessness may be a result of the fall, but redemption restores our ability to truly rest. We can rest because of internal change even when our circumstances haven't changed externally.

That's why Jesus promised true rest:

> Come to me, all who labor and are heavy laden, and I will give you rest. Take my yoke upon you, and learn from me, for I am gentle and lowly in heart, and you will find rest for your souls. For my yoke is easy, and my burden is light. (Matthew 11:28–30)

Rest for your souls. Jesus walked among people who knew well the yoke of slavery, the burden of rules and restrictions imposed on them by religious leaders, and the heavy weight and unattainable holiness of God's law. The law was meant to lead them to the Savior . . . right to Jesus, in fact. Jesus offered freedom where there was bondage, spiritual rest where there was endless striving, and a sigh of relief where only anxious restlessness existed before.

His Word is true for me and you today as well—the offer still stands. When we put our hope in Jesus, we trade restless feelings about our *not yets* and *not enoughs* for his *already* and *all-satisfying.* We trade the burden of trying to access what we think we're missing for the rest that comes when we receive what God fully provides.

Does this mean we just accept our lives as is and aspire to nothing more? Of course not! It simply means that we don't have to wait for more and better in order to fully rest. We can be at rest right where we are because our ability to "be still, and know that [he is] God" (Psalm 46:10) is not dependent on whether our circumstances feel restful or light. It's wholly dependent on where we turn for true rest. God made us to need him, to turn to him for the rest we seek. It's an active response to the restlessness we may feel.

We are made by God, for God, and to be satisfied in God. That's what Augustine was saying when he wrote, "You have made us for yourself, and our heart is restless until it rests in thee."[2]

Naming the Source

I don't know about you, but when I come home from a long day, the first thing I do is drop my bags at the door, take off my shoes, and change into comfortable clothes. I remove everything that's weighed me down all day because I'm home and ready to rest.

I can't simultaneously choose to rest and work frantically. I can't be at rest and pace the floor at the same time. It's not resting if I'm also scheming, manipulating, or strategizing a way to get something I want. That's not resting. Resting in God means choosing to lay down our self-reliant ways of accessing more. God wants us to rely fully on him and his grace and, therefore, be at rest.

The truth is, if you and I are angsty and restless about the right nows of our lives, it has less to do with a desire for progress and more to do with a doubt that our present reality is purpose ful for what is not yet fulfilled. In other words, our restlessness is more of a heart issue than a problem-solving issue.

What I really need during my most restless seasons, and what I continue to need day by day, is to see my current circumstances the way God does. I need to align my perspective with his and to call on him now, to trust him now, to walk with him now, to obey him now.

This might mean you and I need to stop looking for a remedy for our restlessness and press into it instead.

Okay, but how?

Simply put, I think it starts with being honest about why we're restless, naming what we think we don't have, and talking to the Lord about those not yets in our lives. We can't do the work in our own hearts or with God if we're not honest about what we're really struggling with or what we think is missing in our lives. Worldly counsel might suggest that we name what we want as a way to manifest and achieve goals for ourselves, but what I'm proposing is completely different.

We're not naming the source of our restless longings to will into being what we think we deserve. Instead, we're naming the source of our restless longings in order to see them through the lens of God's story of redemption—through gospel glasses, if you will. Only through this lens will we find the true remedy for our discontent and longing for what's unfulfilled, not yet, or not enough.

Let me offer you a simple rubric for self-assessment:

1. What circumstance is causing my restlessness?
2. What underlying identity or self-worth issues am I struggling with?
3. According to God's Word and wisdom, is the remedy for what I need found in myself or in him? In my efforts or in God's work?
4. How can I stop scrambling and start resting right where I am?

Here's an example of an honest confession of restlessness from my early motherhood days:

> *God, I'm restless for more than the thankless job of changing diapers, cleaning the house, and breaking up toddler fights every day. I want to be appreciated for what I'm good at, and I don't feel good at this mundane and tedious work! I have gifts that I'm not getting to use, and I don't think I'll feel fulfilled until I do.*

And here's the way I'd assess my feelings as they arise:

1. **What circumstance is causing my restlessness?** The life circumstance causing my restlessness is the weariness and mundane everydayness of these little years. I feel like I have no life of my own.
2. **What underlying identity or self-worth issues am I struggling with?** I'm believing that my value comes from a paycheck or approval from others.

3. **According to God's Word and wisdom, is the remedy for what I need found in myself or in him? In my efforts or in God's work?** My worth and value come from what God says about me, not from what I do for him. My identity is in him when I've been saved by grace through faith. That means my life is not my own. He created me (as a masterpiece!), and he has a purpose for my life—that I might walk in the grace that saved me. My approval will never come from what others think of me but from what God says about me.

4. **How can I stop scrambling and start resting right where I am?** I can be on the lookout for how God will use all the gifts he's given me, but I can trust that what I've been given to do today is also valuable and purposeful. The value assigned to how I use my giftings is not dependent on paychecks or approval, so I can choose to use them now, even in my current context as a mom to young children, right where I am.

This little exercise in preaching and applying the truth to myself changed my life and carried me through the most restless seasons. It exposed the ways in which some of my restless thoughts were idolatrous and a form of worshiping my own dreams and aspirations instead of the God who created me with the giftings I desired to use. But it also helped me to process what I was longing for, and when I chose to put my trust in him again, I learned to be steadfast in my identity in Christ while simultaneously using my giftings in ways I wouldn't have planned for myself.

I encourage you to grab your journal and walk through

> God wants your heart more than he wants your dreams to come true.

these questions yourself. I promise, it'll help clear away the foggy feeling of restlessness and bring some clarity to what you're really wrestling with.

Remember: God wants your heart more than he wants your dreams to come true.

Reframing Your Not-Yet-Wonderful Season

If our hearts are what God is truly after, then here's the paradigm shift that will transform our restlessness right now: feeling restless and unsatisfied is exactly where we need to be in order for God to shape us and take us where he wants us to go.

If our desire is to experience more of God's purposes and plans for our lives, then a posture of rest in the God we trust—free and unhindered—is exactly what we must cultivate right now.

Let that truth reframe the way you see your current not-yet-wonderful season. It's okay if you're not suddenly carefree, content, and confident of God's desires and plans for you. Just promise me you'll draw a line from your restlessness to the root cause of your unrest. You'll see it if you peel back the layers to the questions you're really asking and the fears you're trying to still. God will meet you right where you are in the messy middle of all that. I promise.

Friend, restlessness is not a puzzle for us to solve on our own; it's an invitation from God to find answers in him, to press in and discover who he is and why we can rest in him. It's all about what he's doing when you can't tell that anything extraordinary is happening at all. If you don't yet have eyes to see it, don't fret. He's inviting us to step in just a little closer to him each time.

TRUTH TO PRESS INTO

You were made to rest in him.

A LITURGY FOR WHEN YOU LONG
FOR SOMETHING NEW

I'm restless, O God, at night and in the light,
in my thoughts and in the secret places
of my heart's desires.
I toss and turn as if resisting sleep,
like one who has not found what she's looking for.
But you may be found,
and I have been found by you.
For those you find and rescue,
the yoke of slavery to sin is no more.
Rest is not just a possibility but a promise.
So I bring everything that is unresolved, imperfect,
and not how it ought to be,
and I set it before your throne,
where you are seated,
at rest,
not standing anxiously,
to see how it will all turn out.
Calm my anxious heart, O Lord.
Deposit within me the peace
that passes understanding
so that, should I be tossed about
in life's storms, I will find rest for my soul
in the raft of your sure salvation.
I will rest in thee; let me rest in thee.
Amen.

Chapter 3

Hidden Doesn't
Mean Forgotten

Years before I became a mom, I almost opened a tiny art gallery and gift shop to showcase my work in an empty loft space made available to me. It felt too daunting at the time, so I didn't pursue it. Instead, I spent my days off from a retail job watching Oprah grant wishes and make dreams come true on a small television screen. I felt simultaneously so happy for those who were about to realize their dreams and yet so defeated, wondering if my creative pursuits would ever come out of hiding. I was twenty-four, newly married, with a fine arts degree and an unfinished seminary degree.

A few years later, I was in full-time ministry with Troy and expecting our first son, kicking off that ambitious decade-plus of bootstrapping, kick-starting, and ministry-building in the Simons household. I was honored to stand with and work alongside Troy in all our public endeavors, but I couldn't help seeing the glaring disparity in our realities: his life was full of visible ministry while my life felt entirely hidden.

Hidden from public ministry, hidden from my potential, hidden at home with laundry and meal prep, hidden by the limitations of a season that felt like closed doors instead of big opportunities.

Sure, I had giftings. And, oh, did I long to see them flourish in big ways for God's kingdom. Missions! Leadership! The arts! Business! I was ready to pursue that tiny art gallery and wished I had when given the chance. I had big ideas for impacting the world with my passion and skills, but the opportunities God was giving me at that time were ones in obscurity, away from the limelight, grand openings, or the internet success I imagined as meaningful.

No one enjoys being hidden, right? Most people don't volunteer to be small, obscure, or unknown. It's not typical for us to clamor to use our giftings for the benefit of five people when five thousand seems so much more fruitful. And, thanks to social media, there are myriad opportunities to see others taking their giftings further, faster, and more fruitfully than we are in our ordinary lives.

I still remember discovering sometime during the early 2000s that ordinary women like me were blogging. I was perusing a magazine while walking on the treadmill at the gym (when you're a desperate young mom, just a few precious moments of alone time is worth it, even if you're generally averse to exercise). I read about a female blogger who was writing about her everyday life, weaving creative endeavors, musings, insights, and a glimpse of the ordinary into a personal blog.

She was clever, charming, and innovative. She was a trailblazer, so much so that I was reading about her during my one hour reprieve from my mundane life. Her story both delighted me and made me miserable. I was thrilled that women just like me were beginning to tell their stories without network TV or publicity. But I also felt a strange twinge of misery as I imagined that I was already behind, too late to the party, and too hidden in the trenches of all my responsibilities to even consider telling my story to the masses.

But therein was the issue: I assumed that the value of telling my story was determined by how many it would reach.

It wasn't fame I was after; it was impact. I longed to matter. I wanted my days to count for something more than the mundane tasks I was buried under: sorting socks, making appointments, unloading the dishwasher, removing stains from the carpet. This was not the life of purpose I longed for or imagined as a young seminarian several years prior.

In a world where influence is often measured by downloads, impressions, and followers on a platform, hiddenness is hardly lauded as the vehicle by which we pursue influence. One might be tempted to ask, "Do my life and ideas matter without airtime, platform, notoriety, or a microphone? Do my giftings bear significance if only known or felt by a few?"

Perhaps your hiddenness stems from an unending list of tasks: perpetual meetings, clearing emails, filing taxes, driving in traffic, doing your job, and all the domestic to-dos that pile up day after day. Some of us feel hidden due to caring for elderly parents or young children who require most of our time and energy. Maybe you've experienced health limitations that leave you feeling benched. Or perhaps your life story just isn't turning out the way you hoped or expected, and the hidden season you're in feels fruitless.

But what if the hidden years—the seasons when we think our labors go unnoticed, when we feel benched by our limitations, when doors we expect to be open are shut instead, or when our giftings seem forgotten, wasted, or entirely invisible while our contributions feel small, insignificant, and simply *hidden*—proved more purposeful than we could ever imagine?

What if we embraced the hidden years?

What if we welcomed hiddenness as much as we pursued visibility?

Visibility, multiplication, and platform aren't the only roads that lead to impact. Embracing hiddenness may seem like a countercultural and counterintuitive path toward significance in our present age, but God has regularly used hidden years as a tool for his redemptive purposes in the lives of his people.

From Obscurity to Visibility

Consider how often in Scripture we see faithful men and women who were seemingly hidden from their full potential yet not forgotten by God. Remember David, who was promised the throne of Israel yet forced to run for years from his adversary, King Saul, hiding in caves and removed from the position and prominence he was promised?

Or what about the Samaritan woman who met Jesus at the

What if we welcomed hiddenness as much as we pursued visibility?

well in John 4? She was so isolated and hidden from her community that she drew water during the heat of the day when no one else would choose to go.

We read about a woman named Hannah in 1 Samuel. Longing for a son, she was hidden because of years of barrenness, which culturally would have left her feeling ashamed and worthless.

Or what about Jesus himself? God's own Son spent all but three of his thirty-three years of life in obscurity, hidden from public ministry. There were no crowds following him around. No public platform and no popularity. As far as we know from Scripture, Jesus was a carpenter's son, faithful to his family and community, hidden from the world until God's appointed time.

Were the hidden years for these men and women used by God? Did they play a significant role in God's plan? Yes!

David's hidden years proved extremely fruitful as God used those circumstances to bring about the many psalms of worship, lament, and surrender that serve us, the church, today. God used David's hidden years to prepare an imperfect man for an earthly throne—a throne that would one day usher in a forever King.

The woman at the well? Her hiddenness ultimately ushered her into a place of surrender to and worship of Jesus, her Savior. She went from hiding from the townspeople to becoming an evangelist in her community: "Many Samaritans from that town believed in him because of the woman's testimony" (John 4:39).

And Hannah's season of hiddenness—obscurity in a culture where a woman's worth was determined by her ability to bear children—turned her heart to the Lord with diligent and desperate prayers. Hannah sought comfort in God when she suffered shame in her barrenness. In time, God gave Hannah a son—who would become the first prophet—named Samuel. His name literally means "heard by God," and his arrival meant Hannah was hidden no more.

And how were Jesus' thirty years of obscurity purposeful? He studied, worked, and laughed with friends. He prepared for ministry, served his family, contributed to his community, and experienced adolescence. He cared for people and knew what it was to feel hungry. Jesus lived an ordinary life on purpose. As one pastor noted:

> That [God] would send his own Son to live and mature and labor in relative obscurity for some three decades, before "going public" and gaining recognition as an influential teacher, has something to say to us about the dignity of ordinary human life and labor—and the sanctity of incremental growth and maturation.[1]

Oh, Lord, teach us to embrace incremental growth and maturation.

When we are on the other side of our hidden years, we can often see God's purposes. The seasons we, in our limited understanding, had deemed fruitless often turn out to be anything but. So many victorious stories of impact, influence, and leadership in God's Word were born out of long periods of seemingly purposeless hiddenness. It's just so hard for us to see the possibility or potential on the other side when we're in the middle of it.

From Visibility to Obscurity

Let's be honest, though, and acknowledge that God's plan for hiddenness doesn't always result in a season of public notoriety or success on a large scale. It's easy for us to celebrate hiddenness when the good guy is ultimately victorious, good conquers evil, the little guy wins, or God lifts what's unknown out of obscurity and amplifies a voice to influence the world around them. I love those stories. But that's not how it always turns out.

In fact, some of the most faithful people in the New Testament were made small, diminished, and even snuffed out by their persecutors. Our hidden, unwanted seasons don't always turn into the life we dreamed of all along. Work in secret places doesn't always result in growth or momentum in public spaces. Our hidden years don't always unfurl into visible impact.

Jon Bloom, teacher and cofounder of Desiring God, wrote, "Sometimes faithfulness to God and his word sets us on a course where circumstances get worse, not better. It is then that knowing God's promises and his ways are crucial. Faith in God's future grace for us is what sustains us in those desperate moments."[2]

These moments, this obscurity—they're meant not to discourage you but to build you up. The truth is, God often uses obscurity as much as he employs visibility, if not more.

Consider Paul's story. Confined to a prison cell at the peak of his ministry and missionary work, he was hidden away for the remainder of his years . . . in chains, isolated and alone. Paul went from known and visible to a jail cell. But from that jail cell, he loved and shepherded believers from his place of hiddenness.

There's also the apostle John. He was exiled to the island of Patmos at the end of his life, but while he was there, he received from God what became the book of Revelation. That revelation tells us about God's complete victory over death, his ultimate rule and reign, and his plan to bring us to himself for eternity! God chose to reveal how he will finish what he started to a man who had lost all influence by worldly standards.

Neither Paul nor John could've known the impact of their days when God moved them from visibility to obscurity. They didn't know that generation after generation would one day know God's heart for his own glory and for his people through their obedience. They simply trusted God and stayed faithful where they were, whether public or hidden.

God used the hidden years of these men—the kind of hiddenness the world would describe as wasted, full of untapped potential, and lacking impact—in immeasurable ways they could not have known or fully anticipated. You and I are blessed on account of the fruit born from their hidden years!

Embracing Hiddenness

Are you prepared to stay hidden or to welcome hiddenness should it become a reality? Whether you're in the midst of such a season right now or not, we will all eventually experience some form of hiddenness.

It's easy to believe that, in order for God to use us, our trajectory must go from small to big, from unrecognized to widely familiar, from obscurity to fame. And if we believe that large followings, big stages, or bestselling books are required for a life of impact, we'll spend our days trying to pull ourselves out of hiddenness and into the limelight.

This brings me back to the questions: What if we embraced the hidden years because our lives are hidden in Christ? What if we welcomed hiddenness as much as we pursued visibility?

What if God is raising up leaders who will influence and change the world without the biggest stages, away from the bright lights, and unaided by social media platforms, viral content, or attractive skills and talents because their lives in Christ set them apart? What if God can accomplish all that he wills without bowing to algorithms, the best hair and makeup, or a bajillion subscribers?

At this point, maybe you're thinking, *That's a beautiful perspective, Ruth, but I get so discouraged when I'm not getting anywhere with my endeavors, when I feel like my work doesn't matter, and when I feel like I have to play the social media game to get my message out to the world.*

Friend, it may not seem like it, but I'm preaching to my very own heart here as well. It's not lost on me that I'm sharing these thoughts in a traditionally published book that will be distributed across the globe. Or that I have influence through the social media and internet platforms I've created. I see that and understand the irony of talking to you about hiddenness when a part of my life is known and public.

But don't misunderstand my point. I'm not trying to convince you that visibility is wrong or that obscurity is somehow more holy. I'm not encouraging us to forfeit God-given opportunities for an elusive "greater reach." I'm simply suggesting that if we're hoping for our lives to have true impact, there's a place for both visibility and obscurity—in the big picture and sweeping seasons of our lives *and* in how we steward the daily rhythms of our day-to-day lives.

Here are a few questions I ask myself regularly that might help you too:

1. Am I intentionally cultivating the hidden places of my life as much as I am cultivating the public places?
2. Do I worship in secret through prayer and study of God's Word, or am I only worshiping in public?
3. Do I invest time in soul care or care only for my physical body?

We must view hiddenness and visibility the way God does—as equally fruitful in the capable hands of a God who doesn't need human resources or cunning moves to accomplish his work. God may choose to use obscurity on the path to raising up leaders, voices of influence, and great men and women of God, but he may just as purposefully employ the faithful and quiet work of Christ followers whose names we'll never know this side of heaven. Since God accomplishes his will through both the visible and the invisible, we need a paradigm shift in how we see and embrace the hidden years of our lives.

Taking Inventory

God can—and does—change the world through the so-called hidden places of our living rooms, local coffee shops, and kitchen tables. The places where the mission field comes to us when our friends, children, neighbors, and the hurting pull up a seat.

I see this at my own kitchen table. My kitchen table is a lot less messy these days than it once was, and we have more uninterrupted conversations now that the boys are older, but when I look back at the last two decades of motherhood, I'm in awe of how much influence I've had in the hidden place of my home. I'm overwhelmed by how much impact God has given me with the people in my everyday life as I've learned to seek forgiveness, model courage, choose joy, and apply the gospel to the messy situations of life.

We can see this same quiet work playing out in the lives of women who are part of my GraceLaced Collective community. It's in Trina's home as she faithfully cares for her husband, who

> God is at work in our obscurity even as he is at work in our visibility.

is paralyzed from the upper chest down after a car accident, leaning on the refuge of God's comfort whenever she grows weary. Or at Lisa's desk, where she keeps an ever-expanding drawer of stickers, washi tape, and cards to send encouraging notes to people she feels called to pray over. Each of us can faithfully steward what God puts in front of us, regardless of how small or quiet the work seems to be. Our stories may all be different, but we all experience some form of hiddenness, some kind of not-yet-wonderful circumstance, in life. And we all know what it is to labor without applause, awards, or approval. God is at work in our obscurity even as he is at work in our visibility.

If you take inventory and pay attention, you just might

find that even in the most hidden, benched, isolated, seemingly unfruitful times of your life, you've been offered great opportunities to do God's work in ways people will never read about on their newsfeeds. Weekly coffee dates discipling a high school student. Playing chauffeur to your kids and choosing to speak into their lives as you shuttle them from one activity to another. Praying over the needs of your community and following up with those prayer requests through phone calls and text messages. My guess is that you've been given more opportunities than you know. These are small stages that have lasting impact for generations to come.

So perhaps I'm asking myself and, in turn, asking you, friend, are we ready to declare, like Isaiah 6:8, "Send me!" even if God sends us to obscurity or hidden years? Is the posture of our hearts surrendered to the places and seasons he might choose for us?

While others strive frantically to be seen, as if visibility will save them, let us be those who freely run toward hiddenness in Christ. I invite you to embrace hiddenness—however God might call you to it. We, the church, the body of Christ, serve a God who always has and always will accomplish what he determines, in his way and according to his time. Let us be the ones who declare, "Whatever you will, Lord—the hidden, unseen, unapplauded—use it all for your glory and our good."

TRUTH TO PRESS INTO

Hidden doesn't mean forgotten by God.

In a world that's clamoring to be seen,
to be known, and to be loved by all,
there is no end of ways I can make myself
bigger, louder, or more recognizable.
Lord, I confess it feels appealing to be
more acknowledged, more appreciated, more wanted.
But you, God, created me for yourself,
for me to know you and be known by you,
to be a bearer of your image.
Not for platforms or stages, applause, or praises.
I was made in secret,
but you formed me and know me intimately.
While the world looks to appearances, achievements,
    and accolades,
you look at the heart.
My efforts may be overlooked by others,
but you are El-Roi, the God who sees me.
The real me.
The messy me.
The me I don't always like.
You tell me I am seen, known, and loved by you.
To hide beneath the shelter of your wings
is not obscurity but security.
Hidden doesn't mean forgotten,
because you are the God who knows all and sees
    everything.
"Rock of Ages, cleft for me, let me hide myself in Thee."
Amen.

Chapter 4

You Don't Have to Be Blooming to Be Growing

Apparently, I'm really not a winter person. Every winter, without fail, I start questioning everything about my life—including my purpose, my location, and my abilities. I live in an area that sees snow for at least six months of the year, and there's something about the short, bitterly cold days of winter that shrinks my vision. I desperately need my family's consistent reminders that winter snow supplies moisture for the wildflower summers I live for.

We've lived in the mountains of Colorado for several years. Yes, I was aware of the snowfall here, but winter—months and months of cold, piled-up snow, and a long hiatus from the blooms and foliage I love—is simply not my favorite.

Winter is when I'm convinced that spring is never going to arrive and the unrelenting freeze will last forever. Winter is when I imagine that everything, including all forms of growth, is on hold and frozen in time.

Does it have to be this long? Do we really need this much snow? Is winter even necessary? It feels like such a waste of time!

You may be asking the same types of questions about the season you're currently in: *Does it have to be this long? Do I really need this circumstance? Is it necessary? Am I wasting time?*

Sometimes the limitations imposed by a particular season stem from more than inconvenience or a lack of opportunity. Sometimes the limitations are brought on by loss or heartache. There's nothing quite like a difficult diagnosis, unexpected loss, or unwanted change of plans to bury you in the silence of a painfully bitter season.

Our family has weathered seasons like that.

I've shared about being part of founding a school in a different season of our lives. This ministry was deeply meaningful to my husband, Troy, who not only gave himself fully as a founder but also as the headmaster of the school for seven years. For him, it wasn't just a school; it was a ministry. It was a place built on vision, long hours with close friends and colleagues, years of research, prayer, and planning with legacy in mind. It was a place where he'd sought to disciple the next generation through his own love of education and learning. And in so many ways, he succeeded as he brought his vision to fruition.

But then came a season of the hardest kind of soil. Weariness and loneliness in leadership collided with unexpected conflict, hurt, and division with those Troy had trusted the most, leading to the end of his contribution to a dream he had invested in deeply. This complicated and heartache-filled crossroads marked the beginning of one of the most painful and confusing seasons of our lives.

From the outside, it looked like we were keeping the peace, agreeing to disagree, and choosing to part ways. But internally, it felt like failure. We mourned the death of a dream. The educational experience we'd crafted in part for our own children was no longer theirs; friendships we'd invested deeply in were broken; and a decade's worth of blood, sweat, and tears suddenly felt wasted.

The man I loved grieved the loss of the purpose to which he felt called, a purpose that was no longer possible, at least not in the way he had hoped. Our family privately reeled from the pain, unwilling to bring any more attention or hurt to the situation. We felt benched, uprooted, discarded, and forgotten. We couldn't imagine what the next season could possibly bring when everything we thought we wanted was rooted in the previous season of our lives.

All we could see were the limitations, the loss, and the life plans we were so sure God had called us to. Was it really not ours to have? It was so hard to make sense of our right now in that season because we'd hoped for so much more.

We asked the same question many of us ask when we feel defeated and without purpose: "Is this season we're in now even necessary?"

Sowing What You Want to Grow

Over time, God answered our family's questions about our unexpected, unwanted, seemingly unfruitful season through the apostle Paul's words in his letter to the Galatians: "And let us not grow weary of doing good, for in due season we will reap, if we do not give up" (6:9).

I want to stop a minute and give you the context of this promise from God's Word. We tend to love encouraging verses like this as stand-alone reminders of God's faithfulness, but there's so much more to receive if we take a closer look at why Paul wrote these words.

You see, Paul was wrapping up his letter to the Galatians at this point in chapter 6, after explaining, in detail, the nature of their salvation—by faith and not works, so that they would not live under the burden of the law unnecessarily. He had already reminded them of their freedom in Christ and how they could only bear fruit by walking in the Spirit. So at the end of the letter, Paul carried on the imagery of fruit bearing and used seasonal terms: *sowing* and *reaping.*

Let's look at the verses just before:

Do not be deceived: God is not mocked, for whatever one sows, that will he also reap. For the one who sows to his own flesh will from the flesh reap corruption, but the one who sows to the Spirit will from the Spirit reap eternal life. (vv. 7–8)

"What does this passage have to do with unwanted seasons?" you might be asking. It's a reminder and a warning that, though you can always sow right where you are, you must choose what you'll sow.

Paul was telling the Galatians, "Since you are not saved by your good works but by your faith in Christ (that gives you freedom!), live with the harvest season in mind. Plant seeds now that will grow into the fruit you long to harvest. You can't see what will be harvested right now, but you can be sure that if you plant worldly seeds, they will grow into worldly fruit; if you plant eternal seeds, they will grow into eternal fruit."

In our family's unwanted season of fruitlessness, we had a choice: we could either sow seeds of bitterness, doubt, and hopelessness, or we could choose to sow seeds of faith, obedience, and trust. We chose the latter—to the best of our abilities. Some days that looked like praying for joy, and some days that looked like self-discipline to stop replaying hurts over and over again. We learned to sow seeds of forgiveness, love, and hope in a God whom we believed (even in our fear and doubt) would work it all out for our good.

Trust the Process

I don't want you to think for a minute that this is somehow easy or will yield fruit right away. In our family's situation, we didn't sow seeds of forgiveness and immediately start feeling at peace with all the hurt we'd experienced. Sometimes we sow what we hope to harvest, and it just doesn't seem productive. We can't see the results we hope for—at least not right away. It's during these times that we have to trust God to do the work in us.

Did you notice how Paul, in his instruction to the Galatians, pointed to the fact that, in gardening, you can prepare the soil and bury a seed, but you must trust the process? Of course, every good gardener waters, tends, and prunes after planting, but once a seed is planted, the gardener has no physical ability to ensure that the seed will grow into a mature plant. Growth is the work—the mysterious work—of our Creator, God.

And so it is in our not-yet seasons. The seasons when we wait for blooms. The seasons when fruit is not yet on the vine. The seasons when all things are not yet made beautiful. These are the seasons when we're called to keep sowing with the harvest in mind, according to the Spirit, even as we can't quite see what we hope for yet.

The aspen trees outside my office window look anything but promising until the first unfurling of their leaves in the spring. And my garden bed appears to be completely dead until the snow melts and the earliest bulbs (crocuses and daffodils!) come peeking through.

It's hard to know that an experience, a set of circumstances, or an investment of time you've made isn't wasted—unless you choose to trust the work of transformation that you cannot see or control on your own. When you trust that work is being done, you stop believing that your unwanted seasons are wasted seasons.

In time, what came for the Simons family truly felt like spring, a new beginning. All that GraceLaced Co. has become was born out of the pain of that season and grew from a need to provide for my family when my husband desperately needed rest. Troy and I had previously ministered, worked, and created together, so this was an unexpected turn in our story but an extension of what we'd always been about: stewarding each of our gifts to God's glory and for kingdom impact. I just never expected to be the one in the spotlight.

Now, many years later, we've written a family discipleship book together, hosted a podcast to encourage parents, launched two mancubs out into the world, and begun local education and ministry efforts rooted in the same heart we had in our previous season of life. And we continue to shoulder the rewarding work of GraceLaced Co. together—me at the helm, Troy shepherding and overseeing operations. This ministry-driven company came as a result of the limitations and lack we experienced during an unwanted season. We could not see past it at the time. But God knew.

We simply cannot measure the success of our right-now season without taking into consideration the not-yet-fully-revealed plans God has for us. We can't undermine the growth that's happening when we don't see visible fruit. In a world that platforms the inexperienced and seems to legitimize sensational, overnight success stories, we need to remember that, despite how it might feel, slow growth is still growth.

Need more proof?

At age twenty-three, Oprah Winfrey was fired from her first job. And some stories report that, at age thirty, Martha Stewart was a stockbroker. At age thirty, Harrison Ford was a carpenter. At age twenty-eight, J.K. Rowling was a depressed single

> Despite how it might feel, slow growth is still growth.

parent on welfare, unable to pay rent and hitting rock bottom. Apparently, she finished writing *Harry Potter and the Sorcerer's Stone* at age thirty and was then turned down thirteen times before it was published. You get the point: progress takes time.

The Bible is full of accounts of people who walked through seasons of limitations long before they knew seasons of fruitfulness. Perhaps the most detailed account of this type of story is the unfolding of Joseph's life in the Old Testament.

Joseph was the second youngest of Jacob's twelve sons and his father's favorite. Out of their jealousy and spite over Joseph's claim to have favor from God, his older brothers sold him into slavery, which eventually led him to the home of Potiphar in Egypt. In Potiphar's home, Joseph experienced unexpected favor due to his remarkable success. But it was also there that Joseph received unwarranted imprisonment as a result of resisting advances from Potiphar's wife. He was slandered and set up for doing what was right! Eventually, through a God-ordained series of events, Joseph was released from prison and given an influential role in the Egyptian kingdom—second-in-command to Pharaoh himself. Needless to say, over the course of his life, Joseph knew seasons of betrayal, seasons of success, seasons of flourishing in his God-given giftings, and seasons when his life seemed wasted and forgotten.

It would be twenty-two long years of wondering how each of those seasons fit together or made any sense before a famine brought Joseph's brothers to Egypt in search of grain, where they eventually discovered that their forgotten brother was now in charge of the entire land.

Joseph spent twenty-two years remembering God's promises, even when he didn't know how his story would end. Season after season of trusting God led him to say to his brothers in the end, "As for you, you meant evil against me, but God meant it for good, to bring it about that many people should be kept alive, as they are today" (Genesis 50:20). God indeed had a purpose for those seasons that didn't seem fair and did not make sense to Joseph.

Don't Waste Your Season

God doesn't waste the season we're in, but sometimes we do. The question is: How can we *not* waste the current seasons we're in when we're so ready to see fruit in our lives?

Well, perhaps we start by asking ourselves, *What are some ways I might already be wasting my season?* Here are a few of my easy default modes:

- mentally checking out until I see new circumstances
- using my time to numb my pain and disappointment
- distancing myself from God because I don't know how to talk to him about my frustrations
- shaming myself for not being happier
- forcing and fabricating blooms that won't last
- not sowing with the harvest in mind

It's easy to fall into these default modes without even realizing we're doing it. I don't think any of us are trying to waste the season we're in. If anything, I think we simply slip into a holding pattern, hoping something will change while we feel stuck in our lack of fruitfulness. I catch myself defaulting to wasteful modes of thinking and inaction more often than I want to admit.

The other day, I felt defeated in the busyness of my current season, which has led to an unraveling of some healthy rhythms in my life—rhythms like time in the Word, physical exercise, and getting enough sleep. I could see how my current lack of self-care and self-discipline was causing me to feel fruitless . . . even a bit like I was starting to wither. Guess what I chose to do in response? I scrolled Instagram reels, of course! We all know how much that helps. I checked out and defaulted to numbing the defeat rather than choosing to sow intentionally. (And, in turn, I ended up unintentionally sowing . . . wastefully.)

So how do we avoid doing this? Psalm 1:1–3 gives insight into how not to waste our season:

> Blessed is the one
>> who does not walk in step with the wicked
> or stand in the way that sinners take
>> or sit in the company of mockers,
> but whose delight is in the law of the LORD,
>> and who meditates on his law day and night.
> That person is like a tree planted by streams of
>> water,
>> which yields its fruit in season
> and whose leaf does not wither—
>> whatever they do prospers. (NIV)

The psalmist compared and contrasted the characteristics of a healthy and fruitful tree in and out of season. The posture of being "blessed" (v. 1), translated from the Hebrew word *esher*, which signifies "rightness" or "straightness" of path, refers to being in alignment with God's ways rather than worldly ways. It's staying and abiding with God. A tree planted by a stream is always connected to its source. It is continuously supplied with what it needs, regardless of the season. That does not mean that the tree will be full of leaves or in full bloom all the time, but it will continue to live. In contrast, a tree that's disconnected from nutrients and water will wither, not because of a particularly harsh season, but because it's not deeply rooted to a source that will help it endure all seasons.

The emphasis here isn't *when* a tree will yield its fruit; it's the preparation necessary to ensure that it will be ready to produce fruit at some point. The point is that a tree *will* be fruitful in due season when it chooses to be deeply rooted from the beginning. We get to choose whether we will remain and stay close to the source of God's Word in the right nows of our current season, even when we can't yet see the fruit we hope will come.

Fruit is not only the product of the season in which it's obvious and manifest; fruit is born out of the rootedness of the plant, season after season.

And guess what? We choose to remain rooted, but fruit is the Spirit's work (Galatians 5:22–23). We can't will fruit into existence.

Pastor and author Paul David Tripp gave an illustration about this in his book *Instruments in the Redeemer's Hands*, in which he likened our pursuit of change apart from transformation in the Spirit—at the root of our lives—as simply artificially produced fruit for appearance's sake:

If a tree produces bad apples year after year, there is something drastically wrong with its system, down to its very roots. I won't solve the problem by stapling new apples onto the branches. They also will rot because they are not attached to a life-giving root system. And next spring, I will have the same problem again. I will not see a new crop of healthy apples because my solution has not gone to the heart of the problem. If the tree's roots remain unchanged, it will never produce good apples.[1]

We cannot rush the appearance of fruit to make ourselves feel or look better. We can't put on blooms out of season simply because we're restless for a different season in our lives.

Do you see it, friend? A season of limitation may not define your season of harvest, but it will affect the way you grow. We must choose to sow with intention. We won't arrive at someday's harvest without sowing today.

Embracing Your Limitations

Limitations come in different forms. You may deal with chronic pain and physical limitations that keep you from doing everything you might desire to attempt. Or perhaps you are caring for an aging parent, and your availability and capabilities are limited by another's need for your attention. Or maybe you know the tediousness of a daily commute—the planning and time it takes to arrive at an in-person or hybrid job where not all your teammates are even present, just to sit at a desk alone, attend meetings on Zoom, and fight traffic again at the end of

We won't arrive
at someday's
harvest without
sowing today.

the day for a late-night take-out dinner, only to do it all over again. You can't help but ask yourself as you wrap up another day of the same tasks, same stressors, and same rigamarole, *What if I'm supposed to do more with my life?* No matter the cause of our limitations, for many of us, every day feels the same, and nothing appears fruitful in the daily grind, as if we're always running and never arriving.

I remember feeling frustrated with the limitations of the little years with young children when I was a young mom. I regularly felt limited in capacity, time, and mental and emotional bandwidth.

I felt inspired to lead, create, write, express, build, and make things with my hands. I dreamed of running a boutique, making custom stationery, and being an entrepreneur. I loved to counsel and disciple younger women and imagined how fun it'd be to lead workshops, run conferences, and connect with women from all over the country. But those years weren't the right season to see everything I hoped for in full bloom.

I felt as if I was looking over at my neighbor's garden, wondering why mine couldn't be as full of blooms as hers was. I envisioned, as I looked over the proverbial fence line, her garden bursting with color and award-winning blossoms while mine limped along with mostly weeds that had overtaken the beds. I desperately wanted to be in a blooming season, and my mundane life was definitely not characterized by anything that felt like a bloom.

I was doing the dishes, making dinner for an elderly neighbor, and picking up the LEGOs all over my kids' bedroom floor (again). I would've rather been creating and selling beautiful works of art or having interesting conversations with someone other than a toddler. In my mind, I imagined how blossomy it would be to wear pretty clothes and drive into a pretty office, carrying my Starbucks coffee and succeeding at big goals. That vision held my imagination like hot-pink dahlias in September: big and glorious blooms.

But I had been given so much to be faithful with right where I was. There's no formula, flowchart, or foolproof way to know exactly how we should spend our days in any season, but I knew in that particular time in my life that God was not giving me the green light to make things happen my way. I needed to embrace my limitations.

How do you know when you need to embrace your limitations instead of charting a new course? Here are some of my tried-and-true lines of self-questioning:

1. Am I running away from what God has already given me to do?
2. Do I see an opportunity or favor that doesn't require maneuvering and forcing?
3. Will I sacrifice faithfulness in the areas God has already given me to steward if I pursue more?

Of course, these questions are not comprehensive in their scope of self-assessment, but they help me see more clearly whether I'm forcing fruit or waiting on fruit.

During that same season of waiting and wanting, I started collecting houseplants, which did more than add life to my home; it taught me an unexpected lesson. When we care for houseplants, we inevitably pay attention, slow down to observe growth, and learn a thing or two about growing seasons.

During one of my routine plant-care days, I noticed how much my potted indoor Meyer lemon tree had grown. It suddenly had all sorts of new, tender branches, and little, fresh green leaves peppered throughout the plant. There weren't any blooms yet, but I knew that soon fragrant blossoms would form, and fruit would be on the way. I jotted down the words that took shape in my head as I watered and marveled: *You don't have to be blooming to be growing.*

It was so simple but remains true and encouraging for me to remember even now: God is still at work in us, even in the seasons when we don't see the blooms we long for.

So let's not waste our unwanted or seemingly bloomless seasons, friend. To echo the writer of Hebrews, "Let us draw near with a true heart in full assurance of faith, with our hearts sprinkled clean from an evil conscience and our bodies washed with pure water. Let us hold fast the confession of our hope without wavering, for he who promised is faithful" (10:22–23).

We can draw near, stay rooted, hold fast, and press in because he who promised is faithful.

TRUTH TO PRESS INTO

You don't have to be blooming to be growing.

A LITURGY FOR WHEN YOU'RE
WAITING ON GROWTH

I am not a Master Gardener.
I don't cause the rain to fall,
or the sun to shine,
or the seeds to germinate.
Forgive me, O Lord, when I mistake the plow in my
*   hand*
for a scepter that belongs only to you.
Help me not to dismiss small beginnings.
Teach me to be faithful in the seemingly fruitless tasks,
the everyday mundane, and the hard soil of my life.
When I'm eager to shortcut my way to fruitfulness,
remind me how sweet it is to remain on the vine,
abiding in you.
Apart from you, I can do nothing.
Let me not miss the tasks before me today.
Help me let go of my own ideas of what it means to be
*   fruitful*
and instead look to you for the fruit only you can produce.
The sink-full of dirty dishes, the load of laundry,
the meals to make, the hearts that need tending.
You can and will use every simple act of faithfulness
to sow fruitfulness into my life.
Help me steward what I've been given this day
that you might grow me into your likeness,
that what flourishes from this season
will make much of your faithfulness
and less of my fruitfulness.
Amen.

Chapter 5

Someday Is Made Up of Thousands of Right Nows

In college I took an introductory painting class to kick off what would become a major pivot from a biochemistry degree to a fine arts degree (shocking, I know, unless you've read my story in *When Strivings Cease*[1]). Our first assignment was to complete a seven-by-nine-foot original painting, the largest work of art I'd ever been tasked with. I imagined it taking a week or two, but I was totally wrong. This assignment was scheduled to take what felt like an eternity (it was likely only six weeks or so . . . but it's been nearly thirty years, so I can't be bothered with exact time frames), and I quickly learned why.

To complete this assignment, I first had to learn how to build my own canvas. That endeavor went something like this:

1. Construct a canvas frame using a chop saw and one-by-fours of treated pine, tiny nails, and corner braces.
2. Using canvas stretcher pliers, a staple gun, and yards and yards of quality canvas, stretch the canvas smoothly and tautly over the frame.
3. Brush on and then squeegee gesso over the raw canvas surface, and let dry.

This entire process took days to complete between gathering supplies, constructing the finished product, and waiting for the gesso to dry. Only after the canvas preparation was finally complete could I begin the multiweek journey of creating an original painting.

This particular assignment required an underpainting—a grayscale painting using black and white paint—before any color was added to a new layer. This was to teach us to build light and dark contrast into the foundation of our painting, but I remember it feeling so tedious to paint an entire layer that wouldn't be visible. *Just let me get to the real painting, already!*

After several days of working on the underpainting layer, we got to paint in full color. For the new layer, we were supposed to paint something personal and autobiographical . . . and it had to cover the entire seven-by-nine-foot surface. We had three weeks to complete this painting, so I chose to do a self-portrait set amid iconography and imagery from both my Chinese-Taiwanese heritage and my American citizenship. It was ambitious, vulnerable, and overwhelming in size and significance.

At the end of three weeks, I managed to compose a meaningful painting and cover the entire surface of the stretched canvas with brushstrokes of paint. It looked complete to me, except when I got up close to the canvas. The paint was thin in spots. The texture of the canvas peeked through, revealing not-yet-fully-developed layers of paint on its surface. It looked visually complete, but, in retrospect, any master painter would have considered it just the beginning. And they would have been right. At the time, iPhones weren't yet a thing, so, no, I didn't snap a photo of this painting (to my regret), but I wish I had because . . . just when I thought the assignment was finished, our professor explained there was one more stage to complete: turn the painting ninety degrees and compose an entirely new painting, again covering the entire surface with a new layer of paint.

You don't have to be a painter yourself to imagine the sting of this exercise. To cover what you'd already worked so hard on. To do everything all over again.

After a few more weeks of work, I presented my brand-new, multilayered painting to the class. It was a painting inspired by a childhood photo of my brother and me playing in a stream with my mother nearby. I had conflicting feelings about my family, my identity, and some of my childhood memories. My composition was peaceful and pleasing at first glance but a bit haunting and unresolved when you lingered with it.

An eye from the self-portrait layer of the canvas remained partially exposed. Wisps of brushstrokes formed the shape of my father, painted into the background of the scene, revealing my longing for his more deliberate presence in my life. The layers of dried paint and strokes beneath the most recent layer culminated in a scene that hinted at a topographical map of my young-adult journey thus far. It was beautiful in a strange, unexpected way. It wasn't what I had planned, and it wasn't what I would've created from the start, but the layers beneath shaped the layer that was to come.

What's more, after hours upon hours, weeks upon weeks, my painting skills improved and developed quite a bit from the first day I struggled to stretch a canvas. Despite my expectations for producing a finished work upon my first try, the final painting that culminated from the weeks, the layers, and the practice turned out to be more than I could have imagined before the journey it took to get there.

It was the first time I visually experienced what some say Homer captured literarily: "The journey is the thing."[2]

My college art professor taught us two important principles through that very first assignment in oil and acrylics painting class:

1. Practice makes progress.
2. Every step of a journey is part of the final story.

I want this book to serve you the way my painting course served me. I long for us to press into all the unwanted circumstances and right-now seasons in order to make the most of where we are today. I want us to seize the day and choose to make this page of our story—this layer of the painting—count.

But if I'm honest, even though these are the deep desires of my heart, I woke up entirely unmotivated this morning, wishing I could stay in bed instead of facing my opportunities and responsibilities. I'm a work in progress here; please don't be tempted to think otherwise! Living each day to the fullest sounds inspiring and thrilling until we run up against what feels like a lack of progress and a finish line that is far off in the distance. It's not hard to be motivated, consistent, or faithful when action is affirmed with results; it's the treadmill nature of our current day-to-days, the *Am I really getting anywhere?* wondering, that can wear our motivation thin.

If I could exert effort and immediately see results, I'd likely be all in, all the time! I'd work out consistently, eat discerningly, and never struggle to study my Bible week by week. But that's not how life works.

So when motivation is low in the midst of our current high-speed, jet-setting, connections-building, make-it-happen culture, these are the questions that loom over our organizational apps and color-coded planners:

Does the way I use my day really matter?

What if I'm unmotivated to do any of the things I'm supposed to do?

How do the seemingly insignificant moments of our daily lives really affect our future selves?

It Takes Training

Many years ago, I read this witty remark from G. K. Chesterton, and it's stuck with me ever since: "You cannot grow a beard in a moment of passion."[3] And it's true, right? You physically cannot grow a full beard one morning just because you fancy the distinguished look. And as a mom to six young men, I can also add: a young man in his early twenties with facial hair still cannot grow a beard like his dad can at age fifty. He's not yet *fully* developed; there's still growing and maturing to do.

Chesterton's point wasn't so much about beards but the fact that passion alone cannot produce what time and intention will. It's hard to embrace this reality when we live in an instant-gratification world. You can have long, artificial nails after a one-hour appointment at a salon. You can have long, luscious hair after a single visit to get hair extensions. You can go from being a brunette to a blonde in one afternoon. You can look tan instantly with a spray tan.

But you can't learn to play the piano like a concert pianist in one afternoon. You can't learn quantum mechanics instantly just because you want to. You can't run a marathon out of the blue without training for it. (I mean, if you can, kudos!) You can't become experienced without actual experience, or wise without the testing of knowledge over time, or consistent without opportunities to stay on course, again and again.

The myth of overnight success is a lie sold to us primarily by gurus hoping to convince us they have the formula for fast-tracking results without all the hard work it would normally take to get there.

You may have heard of the "10,000-hour rule," popularized in Malcolm Gladwell's book *Outliers*.[4] It's the idea that it takes someone an average of 10,000 hours of practice to achieve mastery of a subject or skill. Gladwell proved to readers that the grit, tenacity, and hard work of repetition were the real secret to success.

Angela Duckworth, in her book *Grit*, arrived at a similar conclusion, positing that the distinguishing characteristic of people who have achieved and succeeded isn't their IQ but rather their persistence and willingness to keep working on something.[5] Both authors make a convincing case for practice.

Passion alone
cannot produce
what time and
intention will.

Practice is both promising and prescriptive for anyone longing to become good at something.

In the intervening years since Gladwell's book was popularized, though, the researcher who collected the data Gladwell drew insight from has suggested that there's more to be gleaned from the study than a simple encouragement to practice and prioritize repetition. The researcher asserted that ten thousand hours of practicing a skill with diligence does not ensure mastery of the skill. Rather, one must also have a master instructor who teaches the student how to reach his or her goal or destination. The instructor's own mastery of the task and his or her ability to teach it is the real variable. It's the difference between ten thousand hours of practice and ten thousand hours of effective practice, as someone who has practiced ten thousand hours "could be outplayed by someone who practiced less but had a teacher who showed them just what to focus on at a key moment in their practice [regimen]."[6]

Wait, it's *not* fully dependent on our ability to stay consistent and hard at work? We need someone other than ourselves to help us learn how to take our skills and abilities and hone them into fruitfulness?

Sounds familiar.

Luke 6:40 tells us, "A disciple is not above his teacher, but everyone when he is fully trained will be like his teacher." Isn't this the core of our gospel hope? That we need a Savior? That we are not the masters of our own destinies?

As much as we'd love to believe that the lives we long to have someday—feeling fulfilled with our family, in our career, with our friends, or on the other side of hardship—await us if we simply put in the time, the Bible suggests the opposite.

God's Word tells us that simply working harder will never get us where we want to go and that our lives have never been fully our own to mold and manifest. We need a master teacher. And, of course, that's the Lord himself.

Take a look at how the world's formula compares to God's wisdom when it comes to getting where you want to go in life:

THE WORLD	THE LORD
Hustle harder.	Trust God. (Proverbs 3:5–6)
Manifest your goals and destiny.	Everything good comes from God. (James 1:17)
Determine your life path.	God determines our steps. (Proverbs 16:9)
Get what you want by putting yourself first.	God elevates the humble. (James 4:6)
Success equals achievement.	Success is everyday faithfulness. (Colossians 3:23)
Life is short; live for yourself.	Life is short; live for God. (Romans 14:8)
Live for the pleasure of now.	Live for the hope of eternity. (1 Peter 1:3)

THE WORLD	THE LORD
Your life is your own.	You belong to God. (1 Corinthians 6:19–20)
All things will work out if you believe in yourself.	All things work together according to God's purpose for those who believe in him. (Romans 8:28)
You have to hold your life together.	God holds all things together. (Colossians 1:17)

Can you see how different these two perspectives really are? What it looks like and feels like if we believe everything is up to us? Or how we'd steward our days if we believed the wisdom of God's Word?

As a believer, when your someday feels far, far away, the right next step will always feel counterintuitive to the world's formulas for getting where you want to go. The right column—God's perspective—won't make a bit of sense if we don't believe that he's trustworthy and purposeful or that the goal of this life is greater than living for ourselves.

I want you to notice something about that left column versus the right. The ultimate prize on the left column (the world) is earthly pleasure, earthly good, and earthly treasure. The ultimate prize on the right column (the Lord) is eternal hope, eternal treasure, and the eternal presence of the Lord himself, even now. For the believer, life is a race toward a finish line where the prize is God's glory and a commendation for a life lived by faith. Today we run the race with our eyes on the prize of greater conformity to Christ knowing that our final reality is to one day be with Him in glory.

That's why the apostle Paul testified to this ultimate treasure and hope as he neared the end of his life:

> I have fought the good fight, I have finished the race, I have kept the faith. Now there is in store for me the crown of righteousness, which the Lord, the righteous Judge, will award to me on that day—and not only to me, but also to all who have longed for his appearing. (2 Timothy 4:7–8 NIV)

How do you prepare for such a finish line? Well, Paul would say you do it by treating each day like you're training for the race of your life:

> Do you not know that in a race all the runners run, but only one receives the prize? So run that you may obtain it. Every athlete exercises self-control in all things. They do it to receive a perishable wreath, but we an imperishable. So I do not run aimlessly; I do not box as one beating the air. But I discipline my body and keep it under control, lest after preaching to others I myself should be disqualified. (1 Corinthians 9:24–27)

Do not run like someone running aimlessly. This imagery, set in athletic terms, would've been familiar to the audience reading Paul's letter. They would've understood the significance of the wreath—the prize of honor that adorned the winner in ancient times—and how Paul contrasted the earthly prize with the eternal one. Just as we, in modern times, understand that you cannot run a marathon without training, Paul appealed to his audience to consider their daily routine as training. He asked them to consider whether the choices they made with their time, resources, and bodies reflected the training of someone set on crossing the finish line with valor.

What does it look like to be purposeful instead of running aimlessly in our context today? I think it has something to do with acknowledging that we're running on God's track, one he designed and intentionally laid out for us. Running with purpose, putting one foot in front of the other each day, takes discipline, and it takes trusting God enough to keep on obeying him right where we are.

Practically, I think there are a few ways Paul would encourage us to start disciplining ourselves . . .

- by taking every thought captive (2 Corinthians 10:5),
- by dying to sin (Romans 6:11), and
- by putting on love (Colossians 3:14).

When we stop thinking about someday like a mirage of unmet hopes and dreams and instead acknowledge the true finish line of God's work in and through us, we'll begin to see every right now as an opportunity to train for victory.

> Daily pressing on in practice and perseverance are layers to our becoming.

The daily practice of realigning our hearts, minds, hands, and feet to God's Word and ways will stop feeling burdensome. Like the layers upon layers of my introductory painting class assignment, daily pressing on in practice and perseverance are layers to our becoming.

Practice a New Pattern

This idea of practicing what we want to become isn't just applicable to acquiring skills or becoming good at something; it's part of our spiritual journey as well. The consistent call of New Testament writers was to help believers to establish a new pattern of living. This new pattern happens one day at a time through the process of sanctification.

If *sanctification* is a new word for you, don't be intimidated; it simply means to "make holy" or "set apart." We were created as image bearers, to reflect God's character, to be the part of his creation that imitates him. But sin broke our capacity and ability to image him as we ought. And try as we might, we are unable to live as God intended for us without being regenerated, or made into a "new creation" (2 Corinthians 5:17). When we become Christ followers, placing our trust in the redemption work of God's perfect Son, Jesus, we begin a journey back to our intended purpose as image bearers. This is the progressive work of sanctification through the work of the Spirit in our lives. Think: process and progress over time.

Some aspects of our new-creation life are instant. For example:

- Forgiveness of our sin is instant, the moment we trust in Jesus.

- We are declared righteous instantly when we lay down our self-righteousness and receive Christ's instead.
- Our identity as sons and daughters of God, not his enemies, is instantly and fully ours when we surrender to Christ.

All of these are true of the believer all at once. But growing in holiness? Forfeiting sinful behaviors? Becoming more like Christ? That happens slowly, progressively, day by day as we establish new patterns of thinking and doing.

Paul admonished us in Romans 12:2, "Do not be conformed to this world, but be transformed by the renewal of your mind, that by testing you may discern what is the will of God, what is good and acceptable and perfect." He made it clear that renewing our minds with the truths of God's Word will retrain our hearts and hands to conform to a new pattern of living as well.

Friend, we participate in God's work of sanctification in our lives by practicing obedience, by the power of the Spirit's work in us. That's where James 1:22–25 comes in:

> Be doers of the word, and not hearers only, deceiving yourselves. For if anyone is a hearer of the word and not a doer, he is like a man who looks intently at his natural face in a mirror. For he looks at himself and goes away and at once forgets what he was like. But the one who looks into the perfect law, the law of liberty, and perseveres, being no hearer who forgets but a doer who acts, he will be blessed in his doing.

Maybe becoming a doer of the Word looks like choosing to love someone who is superhard to love today. Maybe it is turning to prayer instead of fretting. Perhaps doing what God's Word says means that you forgo addictive behaviors and seek satisfaction in the Lord instead. Each of these examples is on my own personal list of ways not to simply hear and believe the Word but to do what it says. Not one of these actions happens on its own. I don't miraculously grow into these habits or patterns of living; I must look to God's Word, practice what it says, and trust God to change my life.

You see, pressing in with action right now, however small the next step, is the mark of a believer undergoing the transforming work of sanctification.

One Day at a Time

I used to read the Frog and Toad books to my boys when they were little. One of the stories is called "Tomorrow." In it, Toad decides to save all his chores until tomorrow: "I will do it tomorrow," said Toad. "Today I will take life easy."[7]

But then he realizes he can't enjoy today while thinking about all that he has to do the next day, so he goes ahead and completes the work so that he can take it easy tomorrow:

"Blah," said Toad. "I feel down in the dumps."

"Why?" asked Frog.

"I am thinking about tomorrow," said Toad. "I am thinking about all of the many things that I will have to do."

"Yes," said Frog, "tomorrow will be a very hard day for you."

"But Frog," said Toad, "if I pick up my pants and jacket right now, then I will not have to pick them up tomorrow, will I?"

"No," said Frog. "You will not have to."[8]

Frog and Toad must've heard the famous proverb, "Never put off until tomorrow what you can do today."[9]

Even though there's much wisdom in this lesson, my heart asks, *What if Frog is mistaken? Isn't the truth that even if we do the dishes today, we still have more to do tomorrow? That even if we forgive today, we still have to forgive tomorrow? That when we teach our young children to obey us today, we end up having to do it all over again tomorrow? What if taking life easy is far from becoming a reality? What if taking it easy is the not yet that's never within reach, no matter how many things I get done today?*

Suddenly, you see why so many live for their next vacation, the next promotion, more accolades, a bigger paycheck, or some other form of tangible remuneration for staying committed or consistent now. The rewards of ease, status, acknowledgment, fulfillment, or dreams that come true are powerful motivators for putting in the work today.

I think we'd all love to have a formula for how to get from here to there. How to hurdle over present obstacles and sprint toward the future. How to reject the limitations of our current circumstances and accept nothing less than self-made success. So the world sells us goal-setting frameworks and life hacks for retiring young and living our best lives. There are plenty of books to help you get there, and tickets for a bullet train to the life you deserve are readily available at a self-empowerment counter near you.

But my hunch is that if you've picked up *this* book, you're not looking for frameworks and life hacks. You picked up this book because you're trying to make sense of the tension between your present circumstances and your future hope. You want to know what to do in the in-between.

Perhaps, like me, you've toyed with a life of constant striving and a quest for self-fulfillment . . . and have come up short of true satisfaction. Maybe you, too, have defaulted to going through the motions of your mundane everydayness, running aimlessly, and found yourself wondering if faithfulness today really matters for the tomorrow you long for.

I've been there. And if I could go back and tell my twenty-something self about the power of today's faithfulness, it'd be this: *Someday is made up of thousands of right nows.*

I'd sit her down and tell her a secret: Who you want to become won't just happen by default. You're shaped one day, one decision, one ordinary moment at a time. It's the boring, everyday faithful stuff that makes a life.

I'd tell that quick-results-driven girl, "You can't just wish your way into being godly, wise, compassionate, or selfless. You won't wake up one day and suddenly become good at leading, skilled at mothering, diligent at Bible reading, consistent at exercise, courageous to use your talents, or faith-filled when life doesn't turn out the way you hope it will."

I'd borrow words often attributed to the ancient poet Archilochus and tell her, "We don't rise to the level of our expectations; we fall to the level of our training."

I don't know about you, but sometimes I spend my days

assuming ease is up ahead rather than training for difficulty. And then I wonder why my responses to disappointment, discomfort, or discouragement aren't more steadfast and assured in the Lord.

We will usually default to the things we practice the most. But if our practice is based on rote memory and motion instead of being under the tutelage of our wise Teacher who trains us purposefully, it will not serve us well in the long run.

Does God care about how you'll use your gifts, where you'll live, and what may come of all your dreams? Absolutely. But his heart for what comes someday on earth is wrapped up in all he intends for you to become in life eternal. You see, who you and I become—on the soul level—in our relationship with the one who created us is why every layer, every brushstroke, every behind-the-scenes choice to be faithful in your mundane right now matters. It is both for your sanctification and your formation.

In the same way that ten thousand hours alone fail to ensure success, wandering aimlessly through the minutes of our daily lives will never shape us into who we were fully meant to become in Christ. We must put into practice what we hope to become. And by the grace of God, we can and we will.

TRUTH TO PRESS INTO

Someday is made up of thousands of right nows.

May I understand time as you do, O Lord.
You could have made the entire world—
oceans, rivers, mountains, and skies;
man and woman, the creatures that roam—
all of this in an instant.
And yet you chose to bring every detail about . . .
     in time.
You were not in a hurry; you did not rush what you
     called good.
You were purposeful with every day of creation
and are with each day ever since.
I need not rush, either, when you have given me
     this day—
on purpose, for a purpose.
The breath I breathe today is nothing short
of a gift from you
to begin again, continue on, trust the process,
and practice what I hope to become.
So teach me diligence and discipline,
especially when the process feels tedious
and requires more time than I think it should.
You appoint what is necessary in repetition and
     duration
for my formation and advancement.
You, O God, are faithful to complete the work you
     begin in me,

so let me not get ahead of you
and not fall behind
because no page in my story is unnecessary in the book
    of my life.
I will walk in step with you today, so that I might be
exactly where I'm meant to be tomorrow . . .
with you.
Amen.

Chapter 6

Chaos Produces Character

It's as if my body knows the alarm is about to go off, so I wake up a few minutes early to stress out in anticipation. Soothing chimes attempt to welcome the morning. *Oh yes, there it is.*

Before I've even moved a muscle, my heart starts racing, and chaotic thoughts start filling my mind: *Did we remember to call the contractor back? Oh no, I forgot to transfer the clothes to the dryer last night. What's for dinner tonight? We can't eat out again—we're already blowing the budget this week. What can we defrost now that will be ready tonight? And what about the conversation we never finished last week? I feel like a bad mom. I need a spa day. But I'm so behind on everything. Wait—what are we going to do about school for the kids next year? And should we consider moving? They say there are good schools in Tennessee. And community. I wish I had good friends here—people who really knew me. Oh, that new family is coming over for dinner tomorrow—new friends? Maybe. Hope it's not awkward. Ugh, the kids are already up, and I'm already running late. Oh, I still haven't scheduled that mammogram or figured out what to do about the roof that needs fixing.* I pull back the sheets and take a deep breath.

Why can't everything just be . . . uncomplicated?

There's an imaginary story I like to tell myself, and it goes something like this: a stressed-out girl finally gets her life in order, figures out a long-term plan, sticks to the plan, the world doesn't fall apart, and she nails it at life. The end.

Do you have a similar story you like to tell yourself? Maybe yours has a few more plot twists, but my guess is that your imaginary story has the same through line as mine: control your life now to avoid the possibility of pain later.

Maybe your hang-up isn't that you want more purpose and more fulfillment in your life. Maybe you have too much on your plate to begin with. If restlessness is a desire for more, perhaps trying to control everything is a longing for less.

Less noise, less pressure, less uncertainty, less pain.

We imagine that if we could just get on top of our lists, figure out our unknowns, decrease our stressors, and calm our chaos, we would somehow feel at peace.

Can having a plan be a love language? Because I think it's mine. It's how I feel most loved, and it's also how I try to show love. I love being one step ahead of any disaster. One step ahead of another's needs. I show you that I love you by thinking ahead and having a plan, so you don't have to. (That, and by feeding you like an Asian mom: Are you feeling sad? I'll make you a bowl of noodles. You're making a big decision? You'll think more clearly after some dumplings. By the way, there are always extra servings of dinner at the Simonses' casita.)

A plan signals that things are calm and stable, with no surprises. That's how I like it.

But as you know, having a plan is a close cousin to a desire for control, and I tend to be a big fan of that too. A steady timeline, knowing exactly which route to take for maximum efficiency, following through as expected, making a plan and sticking to the plan, getting things right so nothing ever feels out of control . . . these things all spell L.O.V.E. to me. I'm only slightly kidding. (Troy knows I'm totally not kidding.)

My buddy Caleb, who's worked with me on many projects, likes to tease me by describing me as someone who enjoys "preparing to prepare." In other words, I tend to act as if it's never too early to start planning and that we can never be overprepared to execute a plan.

Overpreparing always seems foolproof . . . until my plans fail, circumstances out of my control affect my plan, or I can't figure out how to make order of the chaos of my life. Perhaps you also are an overplanning, need-to-know-all-variables control freak. (I hope I'm not the only one.) But the truth is, all the planning in the world can't fully prepare you for loss, pain, disappointment, or the plot twists in your life.

I planned to love motherhood but found myself struggling with the mundane everydayness of the little years.

I planned to never stop dreaming and then found myself apathetic about my purpose and my giftings when opportunities didn't pan out.

I planned to use my twenties preparing for ministry, my thirties for building ministry, and my forties for expanding in ministry but found that all of those seasons were going to be flipped around.

I planned to grow steadily as a Christ follower through hard seasons and then found myself withdrawn and distant from the Lord when I couldn't make sense of my feelings.

When I look back, I can see now that my idea of planning was less rooted in active and deliberate choices and more based on my expectation that things would unfold as I hoped. You see, our plans can convince us that we're more in control of our lives than we actually are. We're tempted to believe that if we can create some sense of certainty in our lives and understand the plan, then we will experience peace instead of chaos.

With this perspective, it's no wonder we struggle with so much fear and anxiety! Our best-laid plans are but an attempt to secure the confidence, predictability, and settledness we long for in a chaotic world. But what if the uncertainty and chaos we're constantly trying to eliminate are purposeful, even if it drives us crazy?

Strategic Instability

In a neurological study conducted by Yale in 2018, researchers found that while instability and a lack of predictability may feel uncomfortable or unwanted, a lack of stability and settledness is necessary to kick-start the brain to learn and flourish. To demonstrate, a team of scientists taught a group of monkeys how to hit a variety of targets for a reward. When the odds of a monkey's ability to hit the target were fixed, he was rewarded 80 percent of the time. But when the target was unpredictable, the reward was varied and unreliable. As the monkeys played with the targets, a clear pattern emerged: the learning centers of the animals' brains were highly engaged when they were unsure of the outcome, but totally disengaged when the results were predictable.[1]

"We only learn when there is uncertainty," said Daeyeol Lee, a Yale professor of neuroscience.[2] "If you want to maximize learning you need to make sure you're doing hard things 70 percent of the time," said an entrepreneur applying this principle.[3] In other words, if we know exactly what to expect and when to expect it, our brains have no reason to engage; we go on autopilot. But when we feel angst, instability, or restlessness, our brains are activated to learn something it would otherwise ignore. The research claims that "stability is a shut off switch for your brain."[4]

Instability offers opportunity.

This means that your unknowns and the next steps you're unsure of may be the very things kick-starting your brain to learn and grow! Rather than lulling you into complacent self-reliance, instability offers opportunity.

The study's results ultimately led productivity leaders to suggest adding a little "strategic instability" into our lives.[5] I laughed when I read that. *No thanks,* I thought. *I've got plenty of instability to work with!*

This principle applies to our spiritual lives too. Doing

hard things isn't the exception; it's the norm if we're meant to grow in our sanctification. While this study isn't uncovering a deep spiritual truth or using biblical research tools, it reflects something of God's design and purposeful care in creating humanity, with all our complexities.

God gave us the capacity to grow, to press in, and to engage with our unwanted circumstances. Have you noticed how aware you are of him when things are hard? How much more you're inclined to pray? I don't know about you, but some of my most significant times of communing with God have happened when my life has felt the most out of control.

We think calm and security are the keys to our happiness, but, ironically, it's tumult that produces what we're really after: the peace that passes all understanding (Philippians 4:7). The stories from the Bible tell of this upside-down way to an unshakable faith, a steadfast sense of hope, a peace that doesn't rely on consistently peaceful circumstances. Let's look at a few examples:

PERSON	CHAOTIC SITUATION	CHARACTER PRODUCED
Moses	Egyptians gaining on the people of Israel while they have nowhere to go but into the Red Sea	Obedient trust
Ruth	Losing her husband and the life she'd known	Humility and trustworthiness

PERSON	CHAOTIC SITUATION	CHARACTER PRODUCED
Esther	Faced with difficult choices after finding out about a plot to annihilate her people	Courage
Paul	Persecution of the early church	Steadfast faith

If any of these biblical characters had tried to plan their way out of the chaos they were enduring, they would have missed what God was doing. We're guilty of the same thing far too often. We're so busy trying to untangle ourselves from what might happen that we miss the truth that we get to know God and are changed by him in the midst of our uncertainties.

How has God chosen to draw you to himself during the most unstable times in your life? Let's do a more in-depth version of the previous table.

Start by describing a recent unwanted chaotic situation. Then detail what you learned about God in the middle of that situation, what character God produced in you through it, and what unexpected blessings came out of the uncertainties. Lastly, describe that time or experience again after this reflection and how God used it strategically in your life.

1. Chaotic Situation:
2. Lessons Learned About God:
3. Character Produced:

4. Unexpected Blessings:
5. Strategic Situation:

Can you trace God's faithfulness in and through circumstances you'd otherwise consider derailing? Tim Keller said it this way: "God will only give you what you would have asked for if you knew everything he knows."[6]

At the heart of my need to control the outcome of my current, hard-to-understand circumstances is an innate desire to avoid pain, loss, rejection, sadness, and any possible sense of worthlessness. Isn't that what we're all avoiding at all costs?

But if God knows what we truly need, and he promises to give us exactly what will bring himself the maximum glory and us the maximum good, then trusting him when we feel confused, chaotic, overwhelmed, or uncertain about the steps ahead should be easy, right?

Except we can't see right through our current heartaches into the corridors of God's mind and know how it will all work out in the end. It may not feel like it will ever work out right now. We may not see evidence of any plan right now. And the reality is, hard things happen to holy people. But if God is in control and our self-projecting, self-manifesting efforts won't achieve their intended ends, then we have to remember why he is more trustworthy than ourselves and our own plans.

In other words, if we want to "know that in all things God works for the good of those who love him, who have been called according to his purpose" (Romans 8:28 NIV), we have to know the God who's got a plan and why we should love him for it.

Do you remember doing trust-fall exercises in youth camp

or at team-building retreats? The idea of falling blithely into the arms of someone standing behind you, supposedly ready to catch you before you hit the ground, is a real problem for someone with trust issues. Hence, the exercise, right?

Imagine that your trust-fall partner—the one standing behind you with outstretched arms—was a class clown. Imagine if he didn't take anything seriously and made a joke out of everything. Would you sign up to fall back toward him with your full weight? Imagine if the partner behind you had a reputation for being a couch potato, playing video games around the clock, and being sustained by Cheez-Its. He's telling you he'll try his best, but he's not sure he's the right one for the job. His arms are thin, and he's looking bored with the assignment. Fall or no? It'd be a hard pass for me. Why? Because when your safety, security, and maybe your life depends on it, you want someone you can depend on. The qualifications of the one you're trusting matters.

Who Do You Trust?

So what do we really have to fear about our future (or the path to get there) if we truly believe that someone good has a perfect plan with our good in mind? There's no reason to be fearful when we remember that God is all-knowing (omniscient), all-powerful (omnipotent), and incapable of failing (immutable). His qualifications prove him trustworthy.

Our trust problem is a belief problem. We can either trust fully in ourselves or trust wholly in the power of God. Let's consider it plainly: trust requires surrendering to the one who

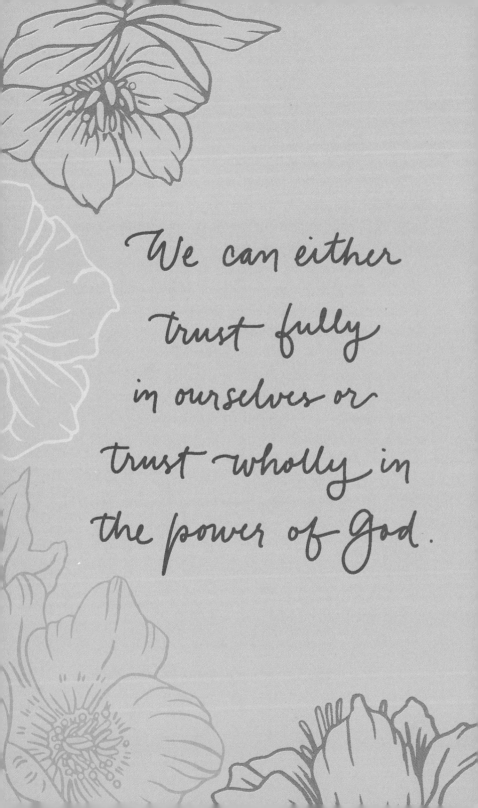

We can either
trust fully
in ourselves or
trust wholly in
the power of God.

knows best and putting your confidence in the fact that he will do what he says.

The whole of the Bible is a record of God's greatness and merciful love toward his creation. It tells of God's faithfulness, his follow-through, his provision, and his unthwarted plans. It'd take every page of this book to detail every way in which God is trustworthy. But here are just a few things God says about himself:

- He sends the rain to parched land (Job 38:25–26).
- He causes the sun to rise and set (Genesis 1:16–18).
- He determines the hour of Christ's return (Matthew 24:36).
- He holds all things together (Colossians 1:17).

And how do we know he has and will do what he says?

- In Christ, all God's promises are fulfilled (2 Corinthians 1:20).
- Someday he will make all things new (Revelation 21:5).
- Jesus did not come to abolish the law but to fulfill it (Matthew 5:17).

We trust the God of our not yet because we remember that he's the God who has already fulfilled what he promised he'd do.

I imagine you're thinking, *That's great, Ruth. I believe God is trustworthy. I believe he desires my good. And I believe he's in control. But what do I do today instead of freaking out?*

I'm glad you asked.

The mystery of living the now-and-not-yet life is in the cooperation between you and God for who you become and how you live. Trusting God doesn't mean doing nothing; it means starting where you are with what you have and looking to him for the results. God desires a relationship with his children, and he is both orchestrating and inviting us to partner with him.

God leads; we follow.

He initiates; we respond.

He gives us minds, skills, gifts, and talents; we use them as we walk in the Spirit.

Wise Bible scholars have given their lives to studying and writing about these truths. I won't presume to explain the mystery of how the holy God of the universe invites us to step into, and be a part of, his sovereign plan, but what I do know is this: we are called to trust God, *and* we are called to start where we are with what we have.

I love pastor and author John Piper's confession in a sermon years ago:

[Trusting God] is one of the simplest lessons you will ever learn, and one of the hardest you will ever perform. Because we are wired—we sinners; we fallen, self-exalting, self-serving sinners—for our emotions to go up when our plans have savvy, and our emotions to go down when our plans look less savvy. At least, mine do. And I don't like it about myself, that my anxiety quotient rises and falls with my insight into how to solve a problem, instead of giving it my best shot and trusting God.[7]

Anxiety quotient—level of anxiety—rising and falling with our ability to control a situation and eliminate uncertainty. You too? I know this is true for me.

So what do we do about it?

We use everything we've been given—time, skills, money, relationships, intelligence, emotional maturity, Bible knowledge, and more—and do all that we can to honor and partner with God. And then we trust him for the results.

Trust is not passive. Every single one of the servants of God we looked at earlier who faced uncertainty and chaos stepped forward in faith with what they had, and they trusted God.

Trust Is an Action

A few years ago, I was feeling intensely beaten down in the midst of trying to fix and figure out so many burdensome issues in our family, ministry, and business. These were heavy things that spanned everything from whether our family needed to relocate to finding a church home, from my husband considering what God called him to in the second half of his life to a deep need for true friendships, from how to meet the needs of our business while living in a smaller mountain-town community to whether we should continue to homeschool. The pressure was intense, and there was no margin for error. Troy and I felt the weight of all the chaos, all the questions, and all the unknowns, and it was taking a toll on our marriage. There was more distance, more bitterness, more guardedness with our pain, and we were quick to call out wrongs.

I remember thinking and acting as if solutions were

equivalent to satisfaction in that season. That, somehow, control equaled peace. I even lost my mind once over a disorderly garage, as if a clean garage would fix everything. What I didn't know then that I can articulate now is that I just wanted to feel safe and secure in that moment. I was convinced that having control over something in my life could provide a sense of stability.

Of course, it didn't. Of course, it was about so much more than making one decision, getting one room clean, or solving one issue. And it wasn't so much about the chaos in our lives but what I was turning to in hopes that the storm would be calmed.

It was during this particularly difficult year in the Simons household and ministry life that my ministry companion, executive director, and dear friend, Eve, started a practice that would in time prove so much more fruitful than we could imagine. Feeling as expectant for God's plan as I was, she told me, "Ruth, I'm going to start praying every day at the same time and specifically lift up these things we can't figure out on our own." She set her alarm to go off at two o'clock every afternoon as a reminder to pray for the needs of GraceLaced Co. and the Simons family. Because she's intimately familiar with all the ins and outs of both areas of my life, she knew we couldn't fix or simply manage the chaos; we needed the God of order to hold all things together and to put all the pieces in place, just as he does for the stars each night. Jesus was the only one who could calm the storm, just like he did for the disciples who feared for their lives on that stormy sea.

It proved to be a small decision with big impact. Nearly every single one of the things Eve prayed for at 2:00 p.m. EST in that season has been answered in some powerful, unexpected way. Eve would tell you that there was nothing magical about her prayers, and she'd be right. But this faithful action while trusting God caused us to be more aware of God's provision. During that season, the Lord provided our family with some deep and meaningful friendships we so needed. Our marriage was strengthened and built up. We stepped out in faith in the growth of the business, and we gratefully hired for needed roles. God granted us repentance in areas where we needed to lay down our pride, and he gave us courage to stand firm where we needed to fight. He steadied our family and gave us vision, healed wounds, and gave us laughter. School, work, church, friends—all four areas are works in progress, but we've seen provision with eyes of faith because the instability in our lives caused us to be alert with anticipation. Our unwanted pain and confusion drove us to a very wanted reliance and need for a Savior.

The right-now life you and I are given isn't something just to bide our time and survive; God has designed our current circumstances for our growth.

I know it might sound crazy to call our chaos and unknowns *good*, but when we look a little further at the way God delivers his people, we realize that God, in his wisdom, allows strategic instability, if you will, in our lives. That trusting God, right where we are, is for our good.

TRUTH TO PRESS INTO

God holds all things together.

A LITURGY FOR WHEN THE FUTURE IS UNKNOWN

I come before you now, O God,
holding my desire to know what's next in clenched
    hands.
My angst over my inability to see the future represents
    my feeble attempts
to avoid discomfort, heartache, confusion, and chaos.
I fear what I don't know, what I don't understand.
But you invite me to cast my anxieties upon you
because you know and you understand.
Your plans were never meant for me to download
and execute on my own.
Help me stop worshiping the flawless execution
of the plan that takes me from A to Z.
Untangle me from the burden and illusion of control.
You're enough for me, O Lord;
help me to believe it—
in my questions, in my disappointments,
and when my best efforts don't result in fulfilled plans.
Grow my desire to go where you lead
and follow your way,
that should every one of my plans be thwarted,
the detour might lead me right back to your best for me,
right where you are.
Amen.

Chapter 7

God's Callings Are
His Enablings

Several years ago, my friend Jennie Allen asked me to teach out of Romans and paint onstage at that year's IF:Gathering women's conference . . . at the same time. I'd declined invitations to do live painting sessions while teaching or speaking at other events several times before, but because it was Jennie (and to know Jennie is to know her passion and get sucked into her vision), I said yes.

I had twenty minutes to teach Romans 8:24–28 while painting at a desk onstage in front of four thousand live conference attendees and hundreds of thousands more online. I was nervous but up for the challenge. I prepared my talk, took notes on my phone, and made a plan for how I'd set up the painting table for the live event.

IF:Gathering acquired videographers with extensive rigs to capture my painting process overhead and with as many other angles as they could. It was meant to be a full-on immersive experience for the audience.

Backstage, several hours before I was to go on, we prepped the desk at which I would sit during my session. I carefully placed original paintings within the frame of view, hoping to achieve a real-life studio experience. I scattered a few tubes of paint for effect and prepped my palette. Since I had only twenty minutes from the time I entered stage left to the time I walked offstage, I needed my paint palette ready to go. My goal was to use acrylic paint to create a sunrise scene on an eight-by-ten canvas. I figured acrylic paint was my best option, as I could blend it and paint in layers, knowing that it dried much faster than oils.

As it turned out, the fast-drying time was both a pro and a con. I knew that dollops of acrylic paint left out on a palette for four hours would begin to dry out, at least on the top layer, making it difficult to break through for fresh paint. *No problem*, I thought. *I'll just use an extender medium to keep it from drying out!*

I added a drop or two to each dollop of paint and mixed it in. I'm not exactly sure why—maybe I was just feeling anxious?—but then I added several more drops. And then several more.

Did I overcompensate for the four hours these paints would be sitting out? *Um, yes.*

How did I come to realize that I'd overcompensated? Four hours later, when I sat down at the desk in front of thousands of women to paint and teach really important verses from the book of Romans . . . everything went south.

As soon as my brush touched the paints, I knew I'd made a grave error. They were slippery and jellylike, akin to grade-school finger paints. Wouldn't you know, the paints' viscosity had basically turned into the same viscosity of the extending agent? Which makes sense, since I had been so liberal with it!

I tried to hide my frustration and launched into speaking and painting as planned. Except nothing went as planned.

I'd forgotten to put a paper towel on the desk to blot my brush, so my friend Bianca had to run onstage with a tissue. And, as I attempted to paint the scene I had envisioned, the paint just slid around on the surface of the canvas. *Five minutes in, and the first layer is clearly not drying. Apparently, the extending medium is really effective!*

I began reading the Scripture passage. *Ten minutes in, and I'm pretending to blend paints that defy blending.* I was talking about Romans 8:26, how "the Spirit helps us in our weakness." *Fifteen minutes in, and my sunrise is looking like a three-year-old's attempt at Van Gogh's* Starry Night. How "the Spirit himself intercedes for us" (v. 26). *Eighteen minutes into my twenty-minute talk, and I'm setting my paintbrush down in defeat and placing my hands on my lap.* Choking back tears of disappointment in the failed attempt to use my giftings effectively, I read the final verse of the passage: "And we know that for those who love God all things work together for good, for those who are called according to his purpose" (v. 28).

"The Lord will use your gifts for his glory, but it may not look the way you think it should," I said to the audience, who could now see that I wasn't going to finish the painting. "When we read in Romans 8:28 that 'for those who love God all things work together for good,' it doesn't mean that he will make all things neat and tidy; it means that Christ makes *himself* our good and works it out so that we get to experience him and his purposes through all things." I closed in prayer and walked offstage, face flushed with embarrassment and heart heavy with defeat.

I believed the words I was teaching, but I certainly didn't want to have to put those truths on display in real time, onstage, in front of thousands of people.

It was a tangible way for me to rehearse this truth: when we love God, he becomes our most treasured good—above and beyond everything working out the way we want it to.

I didn't rehearse that truth until the other side of a good cry that day in Dallas. But when I finally settled down, it was humorously obvious: I, Ruth Chou Simons, working out this truth vulnerably and in real time, was the illustration for the message, *not* the painting I failed to execute.

I expected to glorify God by using the tools in my toolbox, the giftings I was known for, and the time I had invested in planning this moment. But God chose to use my weakness, my imperfection, and my lack of experience to teach the truth of his Word in a way that a polished, synchronized teaching-and-painting session couldn't have.

"Called according to his purpose" (v. 28). Friend, his purposes will not be thwarted, even if our plans are!

What if God is glorified in our weaknesses and inadequacies? What if faithfully using what we have right now is exactly what God desires from us, even when we don't have everything we need?

When You're Unlikely

Someone has said, "Choose a job you love, and you will never have to work a day in your life." I know what that sentiment means, but I must confess that I disagree.

Every "job" I'm currently called to—mom, wife, author, artist, podcaster, speaker, business owner—is a job I really, really enjoy. And sometimes I still don't want to show up for work.

Sometimes it feels like too much to carry. Sometimes the tasks are too hard. Sometimes I struggle with the pressure. And almost every day there's an opportunity for me to question my ability to do any of the things I've been given to do.

My kids need a more patient mom.

I don't have enough experience to lead a business this size.

There are more qualified people to disciple others.

How can I be a public speaker if I naturally struggle with being onstage?

I'm too introverted for a job that involves spending time with so many people.

How do we put our hands to the plow of everyday faithfulness when we doubt our capability in the roles he's given us?

We've homeschooled some or all of our boys at various times throughout our parenting journey, and whenever the topic came up in conversation, another mom would inevitably say, "I'd be terrible at teaching my children. I'm definitely not cut out for that." And I'd always chuckle, because let's be real: I didn't homeschool my kids because I felt particularly good at it.

The picture you have in your head of an idyllic home-schooling space with an inspiring homeschooling mom? With maps on the walls and brightly colored cubbies filled with books and supplies all neatly organized? Just let that picture go. I tried, and it wasn't me. Troy and I felt led to homeschool those particular children in that particular season, and God's callings proved to be his enablings.

A similar assumption is made of me whenever I share that I'm a mama to six boys. I now add a disclaimer early in the conversation in hopes of managing expectations by referring to myself as "an unlikely mama to six boys."

Why? Because the assumption is almost always that we have six boys because we either kept trying for a girl (nope), we didn't know what caused it (good one), we didn't own a TV (we do), or parenting came easily to us (try again). "You must be good at it to have so many," is the refrain in checkout lines. "Good at it?" I scoff. "Who could possibly be good at chaos, noise, and never-ending work that doesn't come with a paycheck?" No, let me assure you, motherhood has always been like a spotlight on all the things I feel rather terrible at. Yet, once again, God's callings have proven to be his enablings.

Losing my temper, raising my voice, getting overwhelmed, mismanaging my time, losing sight of my goals, jumping to conclusions, lacking faith, overthinking everything, fearing the worst, wanting to quit . . . these are some of the things I'm naturally good at, left to my own devices. Not exactly the qualifications you look for in anyone filling an important role. And sometimes, I let the ways I feel inadequate cause me to shrink back from using my giftings or stepping into the work God's given me to do. Do you find this to be true in your life as well?

Each time I've wrestled with this tension, I've come back to this truth: God's grace is the agent of change that promises to make us more like him, which is more than we are on our own. What doesn't come naturally comes by grace.

The Bible is filled with men and women who lacked what they thought they needed to accomplish the work God was asking them to do. These men and women questioned whether God made a mistake putting them in the circumstances they found themselves in, but we bear witness to the truth as we see the entirety of God's redemption story: God calls the unlikely on purpose to accomplish what would be impossible without him.

One of my favorite such accounts from Scripture is God's covenant with Abraham. God made a promise to Abraham in Genesis 12, telling him he would father a great nation and his descendants would be as numerous as the stars in the sky. God said that, from Abraham, all nations would be blessed (through Jesus!). The only problem? Abraham's wife, Sarah, was barren, and both she and Abraham were well past child-bearing years. How would God fulfill his promise when Abraham and Sarah lacked any ability to have children?

As the story goes in Genesis 16, they perceived their inability to make things happen naturally as an opportunity to take matters into their own hands. They decided to "help" God accomplish his plan. But God never intended for them to overcome their inadequacies; he intended for them to trust him at his word and exercise faith.

I don't blame Sarah, though. I, too, get impatient and overwhelmed when I don't see how God's plan will come together. It's easy to count up your resources, the tools in your tool belt, and assess the situation in light of your own capabilities.

In fact, just before I sat down to write this chapter today,

What doesn't come naturally comes by grace.

I got word that something I had hoped for, planned on, and moved forward in faith toward . . . fell through. I thought God had answered my prayers. The situation looked like one in which God's promises were going to be fulfilled. It made sense for God to provide in this way, and I had already begun to celebrate his faithful provision in the situation I'd been experiencing shortfalls in. When I thought God was providing, the future seemed bright and clear. The path forward felt exciting, and the work ahead looked promising. With this provision in sight, I felt strong, capable, and ready to tackle all that I've been called to.

And then the door closed.

Surely God made a mistake. How could this not be the way forward? And if it's not, how do I accomplish what God's given me to do when I don't have everything I need to get it done?

I wonder if Sarah thought these very things while wrestling with her own now and not yet.

Abraham and Sarah waited twenty-five years before God opened Sarah's womb and their son, Isaac, was born. God, in his timing, accomplished what seemed impossible for Sarah and Abraham. Was Sarah unlikely to conceive and birth a child at age ninety? *For sure.* Was it impossible when God was at work? *Never.* This is not a story about Abraham and Sarah's capability; this is a story of God's faithfulness.

———

If you know me well, you know that I don't naturally gravitate toward stages and spotlights. Don't get me wrong, I desire and appreciate attention just like the next person, but the work of performing or communicating onstage, on television, or with all eyes on me is a place of weakness and vulnerability for me—not a place of bold confidence.

I feel well-resourced when I'm painting and creating products. For that, I do so much of the work behind the scenes and arrive with everything all shiny and perfect. But onstage? Anything can happen . . . in real time. Those who know me best (and apparently, this now includes you) know that when I get nervous, all my English-as-a-second-language issues surface. I easily forget the most basic words in the English language. I mix metaphors and confuse idiomatic expressions ("It's not my bag of tea," or, "Not trying to breathe down your throat," and, "It's milk under the bridge," are some of Troy's favorites). It's comical, but sometimes it feels cumbersome to be less polished than I want to be. In my estimation, God could accomplish great things if only I were ten times more consistent, put together, or just plain perfect at my job.

But what if the truth is—as Abraham and Sarah discovered—that God doesn't need our big ideas about our own abilities, aptitude, or resourcefulness to bring his purposes to completion? He will do what he sets out to do; we get to be a part of his plan.

What if we really believed that God is "able to do far more abundantly than all that we ask or think, according to the power at work within us" (Ephesians 3:20)?

What if God just wants us to actually live, believing that "he who began a good work in you will bring it to completion at the day of Jesus Christ" (Philippians 1:6)?

Both these promises are really about God, not about us. They are reminders that *God* is able, that *God* goes beyond what is likely or probable, that *God's* power is at work in us, and that

God is faithful to complete the work he begins in us. God is the capable one.

When I look at Scripture, it's clear that capability is about calling more than giftedness. God calls us to the circumstances and callings he chooses so that he might show *himself*—rather than our strengths—as great and mighty. Need to be convinced? Think about these biblical characters:

- **Rahab**, a prostitute and unlikely cohort in God's plan to bring down Jericho and save the Israelites, is in Jesus' family tree.
- **Paul**, a murderer of Jews and self-righteous Pharisee, surrendered to God his life, his prestige, and his freedom and became the greatest missionary to the early church.
- **Esther**, a young Jewish woman taken by force to marry the king of Persia, was ultimately responsible for saving her people from destruction.
- **Peter**, a fisherman Jesus called to be a disciple, lacked faith and denied knowing Jesus but ended up being restored and called to build the church.
- **Mary**, a young, not-yet-married woman from Nazareth, was chosen to be the mother of Jesus.

God didn't call the strongest, best, or most equipped. He called those he purposed to shape, form, and empower in spite of their unlikeliness. Each of these unlikely people God used in his story of redemption had to let go of their pasts or their own sense of qualification and simply follow God's lead and calling for their lives.

Directing Your Gaze

My guess is that some of us are currently struggling to step into our callings because we've got our eyes fixed on our pasts. It's hard to see through the fog of our own ideas of qualification and likeliness.

Perhaps you're unable to forgive yourself for mistakes you made that set you back.

Perhaps you can't imagine someone with your past being qualified for your present.

Perhaps your family history causes you to doubt your ability to love well in your marriage, lead well in your community, or serve well in your church.

But the Bible gives us a different lens through which to see our capabilities. It often speaks about looking up, fixing our eyes, or setting our gaze.

Here are a few instances:

- "I lift up my eyes to the hills. From where does my help come? My help comes from the LORD, who made heaven and earth" (Psalm 121:1–2).
- "Behold, the Lamb of God, who takes away the sin of the world! This is he of whom I said, 'After me comes a man who ranks before me, because he was before me'" (John 1:29–30).
- "Therefore, since we are surrounded by so great a cloud of witnesses, let us also lay aside every weight, and sin which clings so closely, and let us run with endurance the race that is set before us, looking to Jesus, the founder and perfecter of our faith, who for the joy that was set before

him endured the cross, despising the shame, and is seated
at the right hand of the throne of God" (Hebrews 12:1–2).
• "And we all, with unveiled face, beholding the glory of
the Lord, are being transformed into the same image
from one degree of glory to another" (2 Corinthians 3:18).

I want you to notice something: every time the Bible
exhorts us to use our eyes, it's to turn our gaze from what is
obvious or apparent—what's expected, likely, or reasonable—to
look instead at God and his point of view. Away from our own
perspective and toward God's perspective, where he is the
means of provision.

It's obvious and expected to count up our strengths, our
skills, our resources, and assess our effectiveness and capability
based on what we can measure. It's not so intuitive for us to
embrace our insufficiencies as opportunities to look to Jesus for
what we don't have.

But that's exactly what we're instructed to do.

Our gaze will determine where we go, both figuratively and
physically. We're mountain folks over here in the Southwest,
and when my boys go downhill mountain biking, they talk
about how strategic they have to be about charting the course and
keeping their eyes set on the path they must follow instead of what
will derail them. If you stare at the tree you want to avoid while
mountain biking, you'll inevitably

> Directing our hearts begins by directing our gaze.

hit the tree. But if you look where you want to go, your bike
goes where you fix your eyes. Similarly, directing our hearts

begins by directing our gaze. Our fixations become the rudders that steer the ship of our hearts' desires.

This is a good time for you and me to stop and ask ourselves some questions:

- *Where am I setting my gaze?*
- *What am I fixated on?*
- *What's capturing my heart?*
- *How do I view my gifts and abilities?*

I've squandered too many seasons of my life looking over my shoulder at how someone else is more equipped or more capable to move forward in obedience. I've certainly known seasons where I forfeited the joy and freedom of stepping into all God had given me to do because I looked more to my own natural abilities than God's supernatural enabling. I've been humbled, time and time again, to find that the very places I felt incapable, deficient, or undersupplied were the places God provided . . . just not always in the way I expected him to.

Embracing Insufficiency

But what if our inadequacies stem from physical suffering or deficiencies that may not change? These are the kind of debilitating difficulties you can't easily fix, even with the best tools and strategies. And there's no relief if given more time either.

If you know anything about the apostle Paul, you know he had lots to say about this position of weakness. I think Paul was eager to boast in his weakness because before he surrendered his life and knew Christ as his redeemer, he knew the opposite of earthly weakness.

Paul was a heavily credentialed Jewish religious leader. He was learned, perfect in his religious behavior, and respected by his community. He had every achievement that shines up a résumé. If he had been looking for confidence based on his credentials, pedigree, or power over others, he'd certainly have found it. But all that changed when he encountered the living Jesus Christ. The strength he drew from religious efforts and self-reliance paled in comparison to the strength he drew from the riches of God's grace and the gift of forgiveness and reconciliation with God on account of Christ.

When Paul became aware of his own sin and insufficiency, the religious formula for strength and power proved to be what it truly was: worthless. Instead, he received Jesus' credentials and righteousness.

In the most upside-down way that only makes sense in light of God's love, Jesus endured weakness—he was mocked, beaten, and bruised—so that helpless sinners like you and me could ultimately stand strong in a restored relationship with God. And this is the good news: when we, weak and without hope in our own strength, choose to come under the shelter of God's forgiveness through the blood of Christ, we are made strong in the Lord.

This gospel hope is the anchor for understanding Paul's ability to embrace weakness when God chose not to remove a weakness Paul called his "thorn" (2 Corinthians 12:7):

[God] said to me, "My grace is sufficient for you, for my power is made perfect in weakness." Therefore I will boast all the more gladly of my weaknesses, so that the power of Christ may rest upon me. For the sake of Christ, then, I am content with weaknesses, insults, hardships, persecutions, and calamities. For when I am weak, then I am strong. (vv. 9–10)

Whatever Paul's thorn was, it was something he couldn't fix, remove, or be free of on his own; he needed the Lord to intervene. Perhaps it was a physical ailment, perhaps it was suffering of some kind, perhaps it was relational tension—we simply won't know this side of heaven. But whatever it was, instead of taking it away, God chose to put his own strength on display through it. He didn't discard Paul's weakness; he used it. God's purpose in not granting Paul's relief was for Paul to find the Lord sufficient for the struggles he faced.

You may not be experiencing insults, hardships, persecutions, and calamities as Paul did (or maybe you are), but perhaps you're facing weaknesses due to lack of companionship, resources, ease, or self-assurance. Maybe you've asked the Lord to remove a thorn of fear, loneliness, or lack of opportunity. And maybe you've asked the Lord to take away the thorn of being and feeling not enough.

Because we have the same gospel hope as Paul, I believe God offers us the same provision he did to Paul: his strength is made perfect in our weakness. His power is on display in our lack. He is enough when we come up short. In the kingdom of God, weakness is a superpower. Because in God's kingdom, strength and weakness are not opposites; they are synchronistic with the rule and reign of Christ.

The God Who Proves
Himself Trustworthy

Are you beginning to see a consistent theme in these stories of insufficiency and unlikeliness? God is consistently at work to bring us to greater trust in him.

Earlier, we considered the unlikeliness of God's promise to Abraham and Sarah, and how their lack purposefully revealed God's plan to be the faithful promise keeper. Well, as it turns out, God wasn't done asking Abraham to trust him after Isaac, the child of promise, was born to unlikely elderly parents. In the very next chapter, Genesis 22, we read of God's unimaginable request, a test for Abraham:

> He said, "Take your son, your only son Isaac, whom you love, and go to the land of Moriah, and offer him there as a burnt offering on one of the mountains of which I shall tell you." (v. 2)

And Abraham rose the next day to follow God's instructions (v. 3).

Let's just pause there for a moment. I would be asking, "God, didn't you just ask me to trust you? Do things your way? I waited twenty-five years to receive this son, through whom you've promised so much. How can you ask me to do such a thing as to sacrifice him? I can't!"

I'm certain that the impossibility of the task and my inability to follow through would have stopped me in my tracks. We're not told all that went through Abraham's mind, but we do know he chose to trust God and obey. He stepped into a mission that seemed impossible by all earthly means. He put one foot in front of the other in obedience, even though the task surely made no sense to him. He remembered that throughout his journey with God, God required none of his savvy but all of his faith. He believed God more than he trusted his own wisdom.

And Isaac said to his father Abraham, "My father!" And he said, "Here I am, my son." He said, "Behold the fire and the wood, but where is the lamb for a burnt offering?" Abraham said, "God will provide for himself the lamb for a burnt offering, my son." (vv. 7–8)

Abraham's faith and confidence in God blow me away and confront my heart. I'm quick to fear and prone to jump ship when I can't see past the impossible circumstances or my insufficiencies. But God wanted Abraham to trust him, to believe in his character and goodness, and to walk in faith.

If you've read this account in Scripture, you know how the story ends. Incredibly, Abraham didn't question God. He followed God's instructions and was ready to make the sacrifice asked of him. And at the very moment Abraham lifted the knife to make the sacrifice, God stopped him:

He said, "Do not lay your hand on the boy or do anything to him, for now I know that you fear God, seeing you have not withheld your son, your only son, from me." And Abraham lifted up his eyes and looked, and behold, behind him was a ram, caught in a thicket by his horns. And Abraham went and took the ram and offered it up as a burnt offering instead of his son. So Abraham called the name of that place, "The LORD will provide"; as it is said to this day, "On the mount of the LORD it shall be provided." (vv. 12–14)

God's callings are his enablings.

Do you find yourself measuring your ability to step into your callings with metrics like popularity, approval, resources, and natural giftedness? Are you tempted to feel called when your strengths are on display and not called when it's your weaknesses showing through instead?

Abraham lifted his eyes and looked to God's provision. Can you imagine how pivotal this moment was for Abraham? I want us to notice four things about Abraham's heart posture toward God:

1. Abraham followed God's instructions instead of forming his own plan.
2. Abraham expected God to provide.
3. Abraham didn't wait to receive God's provision before he obeyed.
4. Abraham trusted God's wisdom instead of his own.

What might that look like for you and me when we are given tasks or a calling that we don't feel fully equipped or capable to do?

Perhaps it looks something like asking yourself these questions:

- *What does God's Word say about how to respond to the tasks before me?*

- *What do I fear in this task before me, and how does God's character affect the way I think about my next step?*
- *How has God already provided for me? Am I willing to use what he's already provided?*
- *Am I praying about my next steps more than trying to construct the perfect plan for execution?*

God was accomplishing a specific plan with a specific purpose in his promise to Abraham and his provision for him, and God's character remains the same as we walk with him today. He is still the God who proves himself trustworthy. He is still the God who calls us to more than we can handle on our own so that we'll know his faithfulness more fully. He is still the God who provides when we are not sufficient on our own. He is still the God who works all things together for our good, even if it doesn't look the way we expect it to.

TRUTH TO PRESS INTO

God's callings are his enablings.

O God, who knows infinitely more than I,
who am I to say what is possible
and what is impossible?
I confess that my metrics measure only
what I think is reasonable, who I believe is worthy,
    and
how I think my story ought to go.
And when I gauge my qualifications,
I'm tempted to believe
that I'm indispensable or
that my unlikeliness disqualifies me.
Neither is true.
So teach me true humility, O God,
and let me not continue in a distrust of you
that masquerades as modesty.
May I surrender all that makes me seem likely to succeed
and all that renders me unlikely,
offering each to your service, Lord.
Amen.

Chapter 8

When It's Not
Just a Season

I've lived the majority of my life in the arid climate of the
Southwest and have known both the beauty and severity of
the desert. I love the desert! I gained a new perspective on the
desert after traveling to Israel, though. Troy and I, along with
our two oldest teen sons, joined a few of my author friends and
others in the publishing world on an intimate trip led by Arie
Bar-David, a messianic Jewish brother in Christ who was much
more than a tour guide—he truly wanted the faithfulness of
God to come alive for us. And it did. (It's not every day you get
to visit the ancient ruins of Masada and hear your tour guide
say: "When I was a child, my class was part of excavating this
site. I moved those rocks you see there." Or when pointing out
the cave in which the Dead Sea Scrolls were discovered, says, "I

was in the Israeli army, and one night during conflict, we hid in that cave right there.") My dear friend Ann was writing a book about God as Waymaker, so we also spent intentional time in the desert—riding camels and sleeping in a tent. I experienced the Judean desert that hosted forty years of wandering for the nation of Israel and marveled.

David described the desert in Psalm 63:1:

> O God, you are my God; earnestly I seek you;
>> my soul thirsts for you;
> my flesh faints for you,
>> as in a dry and weary land where there is no water.

A dry and weary land, indeed.

And the hardest part? The desert is not a season; spring is not on its way. At least, it doesn't appear to be. Some of us are on a right-now journey that feels like continual longing, continual thirst, and endless need. It feels like wandering in the wilderness.

In the Old Testament, we read of the forty-year journey God's people, the Israelites, took in the desert due to their disbelief and disobedience even after God led them out of slavery in Egypt. While some deserts are the result of waywardness (like Israel experienced), oftentimes we find ourselves in parched and weary places unexpectedly. For some, it's the wilderness of a chronic illness, a lifelong battle, or a life circumstance that feels like an endless desert with no oasis. For some, the desert is a spiritually dry place you wish didn't exist. A barren place that tempts you to doubt and fear. A place that reads only lack and loss instead of freedom and flourishing.

The Israelites knew this place of wandering well. The account of their time in the desert isn't a story about us, but it *is* a picture of the heart of God for those who wander in the wilderness of waiting, wanting, and feeling restless for more. The desert was supposed to be a short piece of the journey on their way to the promised land, but forty years later, it became a picture of God's absolute provision and deliverance. His character on display in the desert was a constant reminder to a doubting and self-reliant people: since God was faithful in the past, he will do what he says he will in the future.

Have you ever wondered about what God was really after in the desert? Let's not forget, forty years of wandering in the desert happened *after* God's miraculous parting of the Red Sea. The Israelites had already faced the impossible and had seen God make a way right through walls of water to their left and right, taking them safely to the other side and out of reach of the pursuing Egyptians. The Israelites had witnessed miracle after miracle and were promised a land filled with milk and honey, and they were ready for it. But when it finally seemed to be their time, they found a not yet. They would not yet receive the blessing of the promised land. Not yet flourishing, not yet settled, not yet fully satisfied.

Why the desert? Why not straightaway to the promised land?

Because God was after their hearts. Their trust. Their belief. Their faith. And their obedience as a result.

The desert proved to be a powerful place of purpose for God's people. Do you remember how he provided for them in the desert, even when they grumbled and complained? God provided for them daily, with manna and quail to eat, clean water, and his protection and guidance. But notice that his provision was meant to lead them to dependence and awareness of his presence. It was meant to bring them to greater trust in God instead of their own resources.

The Israelites wanted to get where they were meant to go, but God wanted their hearts to be where they were meant to be: with him alone. In Exodus 6:7, God told them, "I will take you to be my people, and I will be your God, and you shall know that I am the LORD your God, who has brought you out from under the burdens of the Egyptians."

Each and every way God met the Israelites in the desert was for the purpose of showing them that they were secure in his care. That they need only to surrender their self-sufficiency and believe God to be who he claimed to be. To trust that he would do what he said he would do and, in response, obey him because they trusted him more than they believed in their own ways.

It's easy for me to question the Israelites' ability to trust God, to follow his commands, and to stop complaining in light of all he'd already done. And then I look at my own life and how I respond to my desert wanderings. *Oof.*

Forgetful of God's faithfulness and quick to assess my situation and to believe unequivocally that I will not survive. That's often the way I roll.

Tell me I'm not alone.

In my defense (and in solidarity with the Israelites), it's hard to stop measuring outcomes by the resources you possess when you've spent much of your life believing your striving will get you where you want to go. It doesn't. So the desert teaches you what you might not quickly learn otherwise.

God allows us to feel barren desperation in the desert so that we might run to the oasis of his provision. We want his provision and the relief his blessings will bring, but we don't want the wilderness that teaches us about our great need for him.

God allows us to feel barren desperation in the desert so that we might run to the oasis of his provision.

We want to trust, but we don't want the doubts that lead us there.

We want to see God provide, but we don't want the insufficiencies that reveal his faithfulness.

We want greater faith, but we don't want the unknowns that pave the way.

We want deliverance without the desert.

But God deliberately designs deserts to draw us to himself.

It's only natural that we'd want out of the desert as quickly as possible. That job that isn't life-giving, the dearth of meaningful friendships, the spiritually dry season, the wasteland of shattered dreams and unmet expectations. *Get me out of here!*

It can feel like the desert itself is the source of the pain, but, in reality, the desert often serves to reveal a heart issue: what we think we can't be happy without. In other words, sometimes the desert reveals the comforts, idols, and treasures we lean on for sustenance.

I'm writing this book a few years after the global COVID-19 pandemic, and I think it's safe to say that, at its height, the pandemic felt like a wilderness full of loss, chaos, confusion, and isolation. For many, it was a wilderness that revealed what we live for, depend on, and can't be happy without.

If you found happiness in friendships and staying busy with social engagements, this unexpected desert threatened that happiness.

If you looked to your achievements and work for fulfillment, this harsh desert ushered in feelings of purposelessness.

If you needed approval from others to feel worthy, this was a desert that left you unsure and exposed.

Anxiety, fear, and hopelessness were natural responses, but the global pandemic also revealed the smaller idols we often look to in our comfort but can't find in the desert.

On the cusp of entering the promised land, Moses impressed this very lesson on the hearts of God's people:

> And he humbled you and let you hunger and fed you with manna, which you did not know, nor did your fathers know, that he might make you know that man does not live by bread alone, but man lives by every word that comes from the mouth of the LORD. (Deuteronomy 8:3)

And Moses' warning to the people for when the "terrifying wilderness" (Deuteronomy 8:15) was no longer their reality should be ours as well:

> Take care lest you forget the LORD your God. . . . Beware lest you say in your heart, "My power and the might of my hand have gotten me this wealth." (vv. 11, 17)

The lesson we learn from the deserts of our lives is that we truly don't live by bread alone. Or any other comfort, satisfaction, or earthly good. Our sustenance comes only from the Lord. The desert may be unwanted, but it is purposeful.

Hunger that leads to true satisfaction. Desperation that leads to dependence. Desert that leads to the promised land of God's deliverance. God meets us in the desert.

God isn't waiting to meet up with you in the not yet of the promised land; he wants you to find him faithful today.

That's because God's desire for his people—for us who are his children now on account of faith in the life, death, and resurrection of Jesus—is to be our God. And for us to be his people. This is at the heart of God's redemption story.

But what if he seems silent right now? What if the desert isn't temporary?

I hear you, friend. While so many of our not yets will be revealed in time, many of life's right nows will continue on for a lifetime. I won't pretend to know all that you might be going through and what unwanted right nows you are facing. And I can't promise any of us, including myself, that the best is yet to come, but perhaps this is the very heart of what I long to share with you on this journey:

We can press into all that is not yet or may never be in our circumstances when we meet the God who is transforming us right now. Because he has promised to one day change everything that is unsettled.

The hope we have in the desert is the assurance that God will never leave us, never forsake us, and never send us to a place he isn't going with us.

So what are some practical things we can do now when we're still in the desert?

God isn't waiting to meet up with you in the not yet of the promised land; he wants you to find him faithful today.

1. Walk with a trusted friend. Tell someone.
2. Feed on spiritually nourishing resources daily (don't worry about tomorrow; receive manna today).
3. Create rhythms that help you remember God (e.g., a good hymn playlist, a daily prayer walk, journaling, and recounting his faithfulness).
4. Ask others to speak truth to you.

If your right now feels like a wilderness, I want you to know that you don't have to wait until you stumble upon an oasis. You are not without resources right now. I want you to see something of God's heart throughout Scripture.

Let's revisit Psalm 63, written by David, who spent years in the desert, on the run from King Saul. He gave us a starting place for our own desert wanderings:

> O God, you are my God; earnestly I seek you;
>   my soul thirsts for you;
> my flesh faints for you,
>   as in a dry and weary land where there is no
>   water.
> So I have looked upon you in the sanctuary,
>   beholding your power and glory.
> Because your steadfast love is better than life,
>   my lips will praise you.
> So I will bless you as long as I live;
>   in your name I will lift up my hands.
> My soul will be satisfied as with fat and rich food,
>   and my mouth will praise you with
>   joyful lips,

when I remember you upon my bed,
> and meditate on you in the watches of the
> night;
for you have been my help,
> and in the shadow of your wings I will sing
> for joy.
My soul clings to you;
> your right hand upholds me. (vv. 1–8)

David used so many action words to describe his response to being in a dry and weary land. Did you notice them?

- seek God
- behold God
- praise God
- lift up my hands
- remember God
- meditate on God
- sing for joy
- cling to God

These are instructions he gave his own soul for how to worship God, even in the desert. Especially in the desert.

One word in particular stands out to me in this list, and it's the word *meditate*. When David said, "When I remember you upon my bed, and meditate on you in the watches of the night," I nod knowingly. Isn't it always the desert seasons that wake you up in the middle of the night with a temptation to despair?

David used that middle-of-the-night opportunity to meditate on God, reminding himself that the Lord had been his help. The Hebrew word from which we get *meditate* in this psalm is the same word for *regurgitation*. Yep, that's right.

This word has its root in the digestion process of cattle. Upon ingestion, the food enters the first stomach chamber called the *rumen*, where it is partially digested. The food that requires further digestion is called *cud*. Therefore, the animals regurgitate the cud to chew it again. They mix the cud with saliva and break it into smaller particles, thus facilitating nutrient absorption. This process is called *rumination*.

It turns out that ruminating is more than navel-gazing. Meditating isn't just thinking deep thoughts but recalling truths—processing them again and again. This definition is strangely freeing for me because it tells me that David didn't automatically grasp and remember the truths he needed to know. He had to intentionally choose to revisit, reengage, rehearse, and . . . well, regurgitate the truths. To ruminate on them. We don't just default to satisfaction and hope. We choose to let the recollection of God's provisions in the past inform us of his faithfulness in the future. That's why God's people were instructed to remember again and again.

Consider this: of all the ways God could have met his people in the desert, he chose to engage with them day by day. When God supplied manna, he chose to provide it daily. They didn't have to work for it, earn it, or hoard it. They couldn't, in fact. Their provision was supplied daily because God desired their reliance daily.

Don't miss the parallels with our walk with Christ in modern times. God's constantly calling us to steward what he's given us for today. Right now.

Could it be that the desert we traverse right now is

preparing us for the promises we have yet to access? Could your present desert serve to root out every form of self-reliance so that you might hunger for him more than ease? Is it helping you thirst for the water of the Word rather than a self-made oasis you might otherwise turn to?

If God's heart is to be our God and for us to be his people, he'll stop at nothing to draw us to himself right now . . . because he is preparing us for so much more.

TRUTH TO PRESS INTO

God uses the desert not to harm us but to form us.

138

O Lord, you made us to thirst for you alone,
and yet, in the desert places of our lives,
we're prone to believe that something less than
Living Water will do.
No wonder you chose to take your people through,
instead of around, the desert.
How else would we discover that you are enough
when we experience
desolation,
desperation,
and desertion?
May I not wander aimlessly in my desert, O Lord.
Give me sustenance from the manna of your Word.
Let me rehearse it, savor it, and return to it
like one who does not forget a satisfying meal.
Use the harshness of my current location, vocation,
or relationships to extricate me from
the false gods of comfort, ease, and abundance.
Woo my heart to greater dependency on
the oasis of your care for me.
Amen.

Chapter 9

The Stories We
Tell Ourselves

If you come to Colorado in the summertime and spend a weekend with my family, we'll likely force you to go over one of the nearby mountain passes with us in some kind of four-wheel-drive vehicle. The narrow roads are unpaved, bumpy, and sometimes a little too close to the edge of cliffs and steep drop-offs on the side of the mountain. Off-roading in the mountains requires some skill behind the wheel and, of course, a reliable vehicle with ground clearance (though one time we successfully escorted a minuscule Chevy Spark down a very windy, rocky, single-lane mountain road after its driver misjudged).

These mountain adventures have become one of my favorite pastimes, though they weren't always. In fact, two decades ago, when we first lived in this part of Colorado, a day spent in a vehicle getting jostled around on windy mountain trails seemed like a total waste of time. My husband, Troy, loved it, but I couldn't understand the appeal. He called it an adventure. He felt challenged and alive in the mountains. He was motivated to see and witness untouched parts of creation.

I had a completely different narrative about off-roading, and it went something like this:

I have too much to get done during a weekend to be spending a whole day up in the mountains. I have projects to complete!

Off-roading is not productive unless you consider getting from point A to point B in six hours at a snail's pace productive. On top of that, it's uncomfortable and dangerous. I mean, you could get a flat tire, whiplash, or fall off a cliff!

Plus, there are no bathrooms along the way, no convenience stores for a bag of chips or a Topo Chico, and no restaurants at the top of the mountain.

And once you get to the top of where you're going, the air is thin and cold! I'll have a headache for the rest of the day.

Also, since I'm not driving, I have to trust Troy; my life is literally in his hands. There are too many variables outside of my control.

I can't have a good time if I'm stuck in the mountains without sustenance and utter assurance that nothing bad will happen when we're out of cell service. I'm not cut out for this. I can't. It's too much for me.

Unfortunately, I didn't just think these things; I'd often say them out loud. But Troy would gently encourage me and make provisions for some of my concerns.

I learned to pack a cooler full of drinks and snacks. I planned playlists that became a fun part of the journey. I brought along ibuprofen and drank lots of water. And I stashed a roll of toilet paper for the potty breaks out in the wild. I took along a change in footwear and a heavy jacket for when the temperatures changed with the altitude.

We planned trips with friends, both for safety and relationship building. I learned to communicate my fears and listened to Troy's safety briefings. I took along walkie-talkies for when we didn't have cell service, and we always had a spare tire and tools on hand.

I changed up lots of logistics, but the biggest change was the narrative I rehearsed. What I chose to think about ultimately changed my mind about off-roading. I didn't just grit my teeth and rewrite the script for what I was feeling, though. Instead, I had to

1. try;
2. consider why it was worth it; and
3. reorient my narrative according to what was true, not just according to my fear and discomfort.

So this is how it went:

I started going—with all the logistical provisions to the best of my ability—with an open mind to experience what I thought was a waste of time. Bringing chips and sparkling water definitely helped. So did listening to praise music. Once the distractions of the to-do lists, inboxes, and notifications stopped on the outskirts of town, I started to look up, literally and figuratively.

I looked up and out the window to the majesty of God's creation. I saw cloud formations I hadn't noticed before. I discovered patches of green moss and living things above the tree line, where you might expect nothing to grow. I experienced several seasons in one day, beginning with the glow and warmth of summer to the snowcapped peaks of over thirteen thousand feet of elevation by midday.

I got out of the car and traipsed through rivers and picked wild raspberries on the side of the road. I listened for marmots. I ran my fingers through the clover and studied wildflowers. I learned to breathe in deeply and turn around for the full 360-degree view when we reached the top. I looked up, looked out, and, in turn, looked within in a different way.

It turned out that pushing past my fears and discomforts was more worth it than I could have imagined if I had never left the house . . . if I had never attempted to change my perspective and my mind about mountain adventures.

It's not that I suddenly became a natural at sketchy off-roading adventures. Or that I blossomed into a rugged mountaineering woman. I still prefer a spa day or leisurely day strolling boutiques, but my whole perspective and, ultimately, my actual narrative about off-roading flipped.

I get to see God's creation in a new way!

I am on an adventure that pushes my comfort zone and makes me courageous.

I am retraining my eyes and my mind to focus on something other than my work!

I am growing my awe and love for the Lord.

I am learning about God's provision and his ways as I observe how he cares for even the remote areas of creation.

I get to enjoy time with my boys in their most natural habitat.

I am making memories, some of which I wouldn't have without being in unexpected and nail-biting situations.

I don't have to be a natural at something; I can be a work in progress.

I don't need to be afraid of not being in control; I can trust the wisdom of someone who loves and cares for me.

Do you see how much of the script about this family activity I'm not naturally good at enjoying and had to flip? Now, almost two decades later, a day spent traversing a difficult climb through a mountain pass is one of my favorite ways to spend the day, to rest my striving heart, to remember that God holds all things together, and to invite quality time with my kids. All because I finally see an uncomfortable situation as an opportunity that's so, so worth it.

Our life circumstances and seasons are more complex than getting over the dislike of bumpy roads and high altitudes. But the stories we tell ourselves about what we're going through have a direct correlation to how we persevere, how we press on, and how we thrive in any circumstance.

My goal thus far through these pages has been to help you shift your perspective about why your right now matters. Why it's not wasted. Why all the layers of your story are necessary. Why you don't want to coast or skip to the parts you'd rather be flourishing in. But if I have one fear, it's that we'd shift our perspective only momentarily and still spend the majority of our days forgetful of the truth. We'd forget why we rejoice, press on, stay faithful, remain, and diligently build right where we are.

This is the point of our journey where I want to pull you close and tell you something I don't want you to miss: the fight to press in and stay present in your right now is

> The fight to press in and stay present in your right now is war; it's not going to happen automatically.

war; it's not going to happen automatically. Yes, we've talked about how your right now matters, how your seasons are purposeful, how you won't find rest and satisfaction anywhere but with Jesus, and how everyday faithfulness makes a difference in who you become tomorrow. But, in reality, we can believe all those things and still not live any differently today if we don't align our thoughts with what is true.

I spend my days leading a team of women and creating resources for women. And what I've seen again and again is that, even with all the resources out there for women to achieve their dreams, find their purpose, and live their best lives, women are still so worn out. They're stuck in a trap of worry and comparison, so eager for their circumstances to change that they miss God's purposes for their present, right-now lives.

If it's true that we take action based on our beliefs, then what we tell ourselves about our present circumstances is more powerful than we realize.

There's a daily war for your affection and attention. And it's constant, because the electronic devices that accompany you at all times are often where the attack comes from. This continual vying for your affection is so ubiquitous that there's actually a cultural term for the people who are doing it; they're called *influencers*.

I'm sure you know what an influencer is, but just so we're on the same page, let me describe what I mean. An influencer is anyone who's trying to get you to join them, convince you to buy something they like, or shape your thinking so that you respond in a specific way (usually that benefits them). It's no surprise that big money is on the table for influencers when it comes to paid sponsorships and ads for specific products.

You and I are influenced by the words we read, the music we listen to, the images we see, and the conversations we have with our friends. We are under influence from social media, church leaders, family members, and our favorite celebrities and icons. The constant stream of input encourages us either to embrace the lives we've been given or to wish them away. But what we may not realize is the one voice that has the greatest influence in our lives.

Paul David Tripp told us who that is: "No one is more influential in your life than you are because no one talks to you more than you do."[1]

You are the greatest influencer in your life. That's because you are constantly listening to the conversations inside your head, the narratives you're telling yourself, and the words you think about your body, your mind, your friendships, and your hard circumstances. You'll never make progress in pressing into a not-yet-everything-you-hope-for circumstance or season if you don't flip the script about your right-now life.

I know that, left to myself, I will repeat untruths about my now and my not yets. Unless I rewrite the scripts I use to narrate my everyday life, I will tell myself untrue stories about my circumstances.

If you've heard me on the *GraceLaced* podcast or have done my Bible study *TruthFilled*,[2] you know that the practice of preaching truth to myself has changed my life and taught me to persevere, even when it's hard. Preaching truth to yourself means taking your thoughts captive in order to remind your own soul who God is, who you are in Christ, and what is actually true about his purposes in your life.

When you put down this book and step back into your everyday life—full of stressors, difficult relationships, temptations, and big decisions—you won't naturally default to thinking rightly about right now unless you practice preaching truth to yourself.

Preaching truth to yourself is how you fight in the war for your attention and affection.

Preaching truth is a proactive action . . . as in, it will not automatically happen. When we preach truth to ourselves, we effectively flip the scripts in our minds. We choose to be fueled by what God says about who he is and who we are instead of being swayed by all the influences vying for our attention, trying to claim our lives.

I have spent so many of my days feeling stuck in the season I'm in, listening to myself rather than preaching truth to myself. And I want more for you, friend! Because . . .

- You are not powerless against the Enemy's schemes to derail you.
- You are not without resources in the most difficult seasons.
- You don't have to let your feelings and fears boss you around or rule your mind.

My guess is that the story you're telling yourself about right now isn't entirely wrong, but it is incomplete. You're not seeing the full picture, and what you do see and tell yourself is likely nowhere close to all that God has for you. How do I know?

Because I've told incomplete, inaccurate stories about my life to myself before too. And then I lived according to those false narratives. But there is something better we can reach for.

Out of Alignment

I've used the word *realign* a few times in previous chapters, but here is where I want us to flesh this out. We can fall out of alignment spiritually—much like our bodies do when something is out of place physically. What are the symptoms of being out of alignment? They're pain and lack of mobility. For bodies to function properly, their various parts must be tuned and aligned properly as intended. Any one component that is out of alignment will cause not just a lack of mobility but also potential injury.

I had a massage therapist tell me recently (after recognizing how immovable my shoulder was and how tense the base of my neck felt), "When you repeatedly operate out of alignment, you're training your body to compensate for the injury with further damage." *Welp.* She was talking about my long hours at my computer with bad posture.

Interestingly, one article I read described how our spines get out of alignment this way:

> Your spine goes out of alignment because your nervous system (brain and nerves) gets stuck in a stressed or tense state. Increased nerve tension will cause your muscles to get more tense. So this extra muscle tension will pull your spinal bones out of alignment and cause poor posture. As

Now and Not Yet

well, extra muscle tension will make your spine stiff and less flexible.[3]

I'll wait until you immediately sit up and stretch out your back. I did the same when I read that description.

Stuck in a stressed or tense state that results in pulling your spine out of alignment. That sounds not unlike our emotions and anxious thoughts. Fear and worry often get us so wound up, so stressed, that our thoughts begin to fall out of alignment with what God says is true.

How do we end up in this state? I think there are two main reasons:

Reason #1: We let our feelings boss us.
Reason #2: We don't really know the truth.

Don't Let Your Feelings Boss You

Let's look at the first reason we sometimes tell untrue stories to ourselves. Our feelings and our emotions are powerful, and we were created to experience a full array of emotions. I'm grateful we have record of David's raw emotions throughout the various psalms he penned. Doesn't it leave you feeling so normal when he uses phrases like "I am lonely and afflicted" (Psalm 25:16)? The writers of the book of Psalms expressed a broad span of emotions, from anger to peace, grief to joy, discouragement to confidence, shame to awe, fear to exultation. They felt all the feelings.

But they didn't let the feelings consume them when those emotions were misaligned with God's faithful works. Instead of allowing their feelings to dictate possible stories of despair, hopelessness, or defeat, they flipped the script on their circumstances and told their own souls what to remember about God's faithfulness; they preached the truth to themselves.

Psalm 77 is an incredible example of flipping the script on a difficult season. The psalmist cried out in lament and sorrow for the first half, verses 1 through 10, then reminded himself of God's faithful and sovereign works in the second half, verses 11 through 20. He went from wondering if he would make it to declaring that God leads and never fails his people:

> In the day of my trouble I seek the Lord;
>> in the night my hand is stretched out without
>>> wearying;
> my soul refuses to be comforted. (v. 2)

to . . .

> I will ponder all your work,
>> and meditate on your mighty deeds.
> Your way, O God, is holy.
>> What god is great like our God? (vv. 12–13)

to . . .

> Your way was through the sea,
>> your path through the great waters;
>> yet your footprints were unseen.
> You led your people like a flock
>> by the hand of Moses and Aaron. (vv. 19–20)

What a change of perspective when the psalmist began to rehearse the truths of God's ways and recalled what he had already done!

If we hope to flip the script on our difficult seasons, we must assess whether our feelings are speaking the truth to us or whispering lies. If we're listening to ourselves more than we are speaking the truth to ourselves, we may be letting our feelings boss us around.

Know the Truth About Your Right Now

The second possible reason we tell untrue stories of our present circumstances is that sometimes we simply don't really know the truth. In order for us to realign the stories we tell ourselves to the true story of God's Word, we have to know what he actually says about these right-now days of our lives. We'll never flip the script on the stories we tell ourselves unless we're given truer, more reliable stories to replace the ones we rehearse in our minds.

And more than just encountering the truth about what God is doing, we have to actively believe that what he's doing is true in us and for us, personally. I think that's why the New Testament writers so often followed a pattern: acknowledging the challenges, speaking the truth about who God is in the midst of the hard circumstances, and reminding their audience who they are because of Christ. The truth about who God is and who we are in him changes everything about how we think about right now.

So how about a quick survey of what the Bible says about your right now?

1. Your Hard Season Is Ultimately Light and Momentary

In 2 Corinthians, Paul acknowledged the pain and persecution he and others endured as ministers of the gospel. He described his situation as "afflicted in every way, but not crushed; perplexed, but not driven to despair; persecuted, but not forsaken; struck down, but not destroyed" (4:8–9). Don't you love how real Paul was? He didn't sugarcoat how discouraging or hard it was to remain faithful and steadfast or to stand firm in his calling when he experienced pressure and obstacles from all sides. But he chose to counter the despair of his situation with the hope of his reality in Christ.

> So we do not lose heart. Though our outer self is wasting away, our inner self is being renewed day by day. For this light momentary affliction is preparing for us an eternal weight of glory beyond all comparison, as we look not to the things that are seen but to the things that are unseen. For the things that are seen are transient, but the things that are unseen are eternal. (vv. 16–18)

Paul called his affliction "light" and "momentary." Why? Because he saw the bigger picture, the spiritual realities of the situation: external affliction, internal progress; temporal pain, eternal glory.

Do you see what Paul was doing? He was preaching to his own heart and flipping the script on what was true about his circumstances! And in doing so, he was encouraging his readers and leading them back to the hope of the gospel.

He could've easily (and justifiably!) said, "I don't deserve this treatment. It's unbearable and unfair." But instead he chose a Christward narrative for the hard circumstances: "So we do not lose heart . . . For this light momentary affliction is preparing for us an eternal weight of glory beyond all comparison."

It's as if he was declaring, "We're all good. We're not giving up. We're actually not doomed, but far from it. In fact, all this junk we're going through? It's actually good for us; it's making us ready for heaven."

Oh, to have Paul's perspective!

2. Your Hard Season Is Refining You

Let's switch gears and look at what Peter had to say about these hard seasons:

> In this you rejoice, though now for a little while, if necessary, you have been grieved by various trials, so that the tested genuineness of your faith—more precious than gold that perishes though it is tested by fire—may be found to result in praise and glory and honor at the revelation of Jesus Christ. (1 Peter 1:6–7)

In this passage, Peter was recounting the current situation for fellow believers in exile who were far from home: distressed and battling various trials. Yet Peter asserted that they could rejoice! In what? Well, take a look at what comes just before those two verses:

> Blessed be the God and Father of our Lord Jesus Christ! According to his great mercy, he has caused us to be born again to a living hope through the resurrection of Jesus

Christ from the dead, to an inheritance that is imperishable, undefiled, and unfading, kept in heaven for you, who by God's power are being guarded through faith for a salvation ready to be revealed in the last time. (vv. 3–5)

So what is the "in this" believers are instructed to rejoice in from that first passage we read?

- a living hope they had because of the resurrection of Christ
- an inheritance that is imperishable, undefiled, and unfading
- an inheritance that awaited them
- assurance of salvation through Jesus

Peter was helping believers rewrite the narrative of their situation in order to align it with God's plan for them and to change the stories they were telling themselves about the difficult things they must endure . . . *for a little while.*

I don't know about you, but trials never feel like "a little while" to me; they seem to last forever. If we're not careful, trials and hard seasons will try to overtake the narrative of our entire lives, as if they're the only stories we get to live. But they're not! And Peter's encouragement offers a different perspective.

Instead of thinking of themselves as exiled and abandoned, the church was to remember that they had an unfading inheritance waiting for them in heaven because of Christ.

Instead of feeling beaten down by trials, they were to remember that their faith was being refined.

Peter's audience would have understood this concept of

refinement in the framework of metallurgy. In that realm, refining is a process where metals are heated over fire until the impurities and unwanted elements can be extracted from them, leaving them in their purest state.

Tested by fire. Refined to bring God praise.

I don't know about you, but that's the kind of script flip I need personally. Here's my default script in the midst of hard seasons: *I'm not going to make it. This is too hard. Why do I have to go through this?*

But as I heed Peter's reminders about what is true, I'm learning to reframe my narrative like this: *I'm going to rejoice in the midst of this. This is hard, but God is refining me in this, making me more like Christ. It's okay that I'm going through this because I have a nonnegotiable treasure in heaven because of my salvation in Christ.*

3. Your Hard Season Is Producing Endurance

Sometimes the difficult season feels unbearably impossible. The apostle Paul knew about those conditions, yet he encouraged believers to set their eyes on what a hard season can produce:

> We rejoice in our sufferings, knowing that suffering produces endurance, and endurance produces character, and character produces hope, and hope does not put us to shame, because God's love has been poured into our hearts through the Holy Spirit who has been given to us. (Romans 5:3–5)

Though Paul was speaking specifically about suffering in this passage, I think his letter to the Romans provides context for how to process any difficult season. Most of us know very little of true suffering the way Paul experienced it on account of his commitment to Christ—beatings, imprisonment, abandonment, ridicule, and judgment. I've not had to suffer like that, but I have experienced betrayal, slander, accusations, and loss. I have known trauma and debilitating fear. I've suffered the discouragement and isolation of ministry and doubt amid burnout. I've experienced bouts of anxiety and chronic illness. I've wondered if life was worth living.

Perhaps you've known suffering like that too.

So when Paul said that suffering produces endurance, which forms character, which gives rise to hope . . . I sit up and listen.

Paul wouldn't have had to reiterate why suffering, hardship, and trials are purposeful and productive if we naturally drew that conclusion ourselves. I know I don't. In fact, my tendency is to fling my arms up in the air like I'm helpless and fixate on all the ways in which I can't, it's too hard, or I'm not good enough. And usually, this happens at 4:00 a.m., when I should be sleeping. Picture an eight-year-old boy throwing a fit because he would rather go outside to play than sit and do homework, especially when he feels very bad at math . . . that's pretty much me.

And perhaps Paul knew his reader would struggle to persevere as well. Paul gave an alternative to floundering in suffering; he gave reason for our rejoicing. Take another look at the passage and notice the reason he gave:

> We rejoice in our sufferings, knowing that suffering produces endurance, and endurance produces character, and character produces hope, and hope does not put us to shame,

We don't flip
the script on our
hard seasons because
we have a better
script of our own
but because we
believe god's stories
are better than
the ones we could
ever write.

because God's love has been poured into our hearts through
the Holy Spirit who has been given to us.

Do you see it? We rejoice in our sufferings "because God's
love has been poured into our hearts through the Holy Spirit
who has been given to us." He flipped the script about suffering.

———————

So let's begin to flip the script on our hard seasons, shall we?
Are you letting the way you feel about your current season tell
stories that drive you to dependency on God or away from
him? Are the stories you're repeating in your heart and mind
informed by truth? By God's character? By who you are in
Christ? If not, return to the Word of God and see what he has
to say about your present troubles.

This isn't some kind of magic spell, manifesting, or man-
tra chanting. And it's not self-help or channeling confidence.
The writers in the New Testament weren't trying to convince
us to speak positivity over our lives. This is entirely different.
We don't flip the script on our hard seasons because we have
a better script of our own but because we believe God's stories
are better than the ones we could ever write.

TRUTH TO PRESS INTO

The story God is writing is better than our best-laid plans.

A LITURGY FOR WHEN YOUR FEELINGS
TRY TO BOSS YOU AROUND

O God, you know my thoughts,
my inner dialogue,
the accurate
and inaccurate stories I tell myself.
And I confess: your Word is infinitely more true
than the stories I so often rehearse.
When I think weakness is limiting,
may I remember that you call weaknesses
      Christ-exalting.
When I consider suffering debilitating,
may I remember that you call suffering refining.
When I see temptations as discouraging,
may I remember that you call temptations defining.
When I believe trials will break me,
may I remember that you call trials sanctifying.
So help me to flip the narrative about hard seasons.
Give me your words, your insight, your point of view.
Take my less-than narratives
and rewrite them for yourself.
Equip my mind,
steer my tongue,
soften my heart,
so that the words of my mouth
and meditation of my heart
may be pleasing to you, O God.
Amen.

Chapter 10

Start Where You Are

I'm writing these words from the other side of months spent trying to discern whether we should move away from our current location and community, only to sense that God was leading us to stay right where we are. Though the area we live in is replete with stunning views and vacation mountain-town vibes, even after a few years here, we struggled to find deep community, felt isolated in public ministry, and wrestled with all that we lacked living in a rural area of Colorado. (Trader Joe's and Costco are a four-hour drive away, and Target is a forty-five-minute drive across the state line. The struggle is real!)

During the months we considered moving, all I could think about was how much easier and better it would be for our whole family if we moved somewhere with more schooling options, proximity to industry friends, church options we felt more aligned with, more friendliness toward Christians, more ease in fellowship, more encouragement in ministry, and, of course, more access to Costco.

I really began to believe that my family, friendships, business, mental health, and outside support (basically everything) would all be better if I could just go from here to there. I pictured arriving elsewhere and finding my burdens relieved.

But, ultimately, this season wasn't about finding a new location for the Simons family; it was about our needing to meet God where he had already placed us. It was about our needing to love the very difficult place we were desperately trying to escape. God could have made a way for us to relocate, and he still might someday, but the clarion call amid our desire to get to where we wanted to go was to start where we already were and to use what we already had.

So we started using our home for dinners, gatherings, game nights, and worship.

We started using our giftings to teach, lead, and serve.

We started using our resources to host, equip, build, and welcome.

The deeper we sank our roots, the more abundance we began to experience. By the time you read these pages, we will have been meeting for over a year in an unexpectedly life-giving, life-transforming, early-church-mirroring house church that is more than we could've asked for or imagined. Troy will have finished preaching through the book of Hebrews, and we will have thanked the Lord over and over that he turned our desperation to leave into a desire to stay.

Sometimes our longing for anywhere but here is justified and born out of loss and pain, and sometimes we're simply restless for more. We're quick to believe that right here can't possibly be where God chooses to use us.

As we've already seen, the story of the nation of Israel is

one of often being where they didn't want to be. Yet their discomfort with the situation didn't mean they were outside God's plan for them.

In the book of Jeremiah, we find the Israelites living in exile, displaced from their homes and far from where they longed to be. God's people were living as captives in Babylon, a place that, in every possible way, threatened and diminished their walk with God. It was no place to call home, and all they wanted to do was get out of there.

They were so eager to move on to something better that God had to warn them against believing anyone who tried to convince them that their exile was temporary. In fact, in Jeremiah 29:10, God revealed that they would be in exile for seventy years and told them to settle in Babylon. He gave them instructions and warnings, glimmers of hope, and reminders of his faithfulness. Instead of offering a quick exit plan, God used Jeremiah to give his people clear, practical instructions for how to live as exiles . . . how to start where they were.

How to start where we are—isn't that the question we all ask? It's easy when you have everything you think you need at your fingertips and find yourself perfectly positioned for the goals you're aiming for. But how do you start where you are when you don't have what you want?

Before we look at how God instructed the Israelites in Jeremiah's day, let me say this: it's very likely that you and I woke up this morning in the exact same set of life circumstances we lived yesterday. Unless you happen to be relocating or on a cross-country trek, you're probably in roughly the same physical location God had you yesterday.

What may not be as obvious is that we are both one step

closer to someday even if we're not being transplanted to another situation or environment. Day by day, step-by-step, we're never operating in neutral; we are moving in a direction because of the choices we make each day. Even choosing not to engage or press into your present season—even that choice will affect your trajectory. Ultimately, where you find yourself a month, a year, or a decade from now, starts with the choices you're making today.

So this is the part of our journey together where I want us to roll up our sleeves and get to work where God has us. Because this is what I know: we can believe that God is purposeful right now and even start embracing it, but we won't experience all God has for us until we actively choose to do something with what he's already given us, right where we are.

My deep desire is to see us both compelled toward living fully and freely, stewarding today because of all that God is doing and will ultimately finish in the unexpected, unwanted, or unseen places of our lives.

Okay, back to the Israelites. Clearly, God's people knew what it felt like to be somewhere they didn't want to be, with a far-off someday (seventy years!). We can glean some practical, start-where-you-are actionables from God's instructions to his people.

In Jeremiah 29:4–7, we read:

This is what the LORD Almighty, the God of Israel, says to all those I carried into exile from Jerusalem to Babylon: "Build houses and settle down; plant gardens and eat what they produce. Marry and have sons and daughters; find wives for your sons and give your daughters in marriage,

Where you find yourself a month, a year, or a decade from now, starts with the choices you're making today.

so that they too may have sons and daughters. Increase in number there; do not decrease. Also, seek the peace and prosperity of the city to which I have carried you into exile. Pray to the LORD for it, because if it prospers, you too will prosper." (NIV)

Wait. Build houses? Plant gardens? Start a family? While living in captivity in a foreign land? Why would Jeremiah's instructions to the Israelites be so . . . well, practical and domestic?

Perhaps the point here is that everything begins at home and in the home of our hearts. Though we, like the Israelites, might be tempted to focus on location or vocation, God's direction to them—and to us—is about cultivation.

God instructed his people to press into their exile and settle in. He allowed them to be sent into exile as a result of their disobedience and rebellion, but they were not forgotten. His instructions made it clear that he had a plan for Israel, even when their circumstances were not what they wanted them to be. Let's take a look at each part of God's instructions.

1. Build Houses, Plant Gardens, Marry, and Have Sons and Daughters

God promised the Jewish exiles that their captivity would one day end, but they didn't know when or how. So, in the meantime, God called them to actively build a life right where they were instead of waiting for their circumstances to change. What clearer sign could there be that they were in it for the long haul than that they start building houses, planting gardens, marrying, and having children?

It was a call to abide. I find it interesting that another word for *house* or *home* is the word *abode*, which is related to this idea of staying where you are. Jesus taught the concept of abiding in him with the imagery of the vine:

> Abide in me, as I in you. As the branch cannot bear fruit by itself, unless it abides in the vine, neither can you, unless you abide in me. I am the vine; you are the branches. Whoever abides in me and I in him, he it is that bears much fruit, for apart from me you can do nothing. (John 15:4–5)

I love that Eastern cultures use word pictures so commonly. In Jesus' day, his listeners would have felt very familiar with the context of this metaphor. When we come across these words—*abide* or an *abode*, as translated into English from the noun form of the original Greek verb *meno*—it's easy to conjure up a mental picture of sitting fireside with a warm blanket. We often default to thinking about abiding as something sweet and secure (which it is!), but the Bible describes it as sustenance for survival.

Abiding means to stay, to remain, to be true to, to persevere, to keep on, to continue, to get in close, to dwell, to be near, to not perish, and to withstand. It means to physically stand your ground and stake your claim. It means not to wander away or give up your resolve. It means to stay engaged and endure. It means to be rooted and settled.

It's much like planting a garden. Think about all that the "plant a garden" command entails: prep the soil, plant the seeds, water, and prune. Work and wait. Till and tend. Sow and harvest. Enjoying the bounty of a garden takes work and dedication. It takes time and resolve.

The same could be said of God's instructions to the exiles to marry and have children. This is ultimately a call to build a legacy, whether you are married with children or not. If you're currently single, you're needed as a spiritual mother or father in the community of faith. Your investment in the lives around you, and under your influence, matters. For the Israelites, it was something that would take years of commitment, discipling, investing relationally, and testifying faithfully to the generation coming behind. The same is true for us.

Do you see the underlying characteristic of all these descriptions?

They're all active. And they all take time and dedication.

Settling in and building a life where you are is a deliberate choice, an intentional course of action. This instruction was God's way of reminding his people that obedience was first an offering of the heart. It was a way for them to say they trusted God, to confidently proclaim that home is where your heart— not where your house—is.

God's desire all along was for the hearts of his people to remain with him, their God. This is the same desire we see in the New Testament, the same desire he has for us today. Building a physical house, planting a physical garden, marrying, and having children were ways for the exiled Jews to establish themselves where God had placed them, but they were also reminders to them that even while far from a place they could call home, they could be established with God, in obedience to God . . . even while displaced in exile.

I think that some of us (and by "some of us," I mean myself) never get started making the most of where we are because we can't get past where we think we should be. We want to be

Start Where You Are

mentors but worry we won't have the answers for the messy life issues. We want to disciple our kids at home, but we envision perfect rows of children with hands on their laps and attitudes in check. We picture husbands who never miss a beat and always lead the way we would. We want family gatherings but anticipate the inevitable frustrations. We want to serve at church only if we get to use our giftings the way we think we ought.

If it can't be done perfectly, I don't want to do it at all.

But the work of cultivation isn't going to look beautiful and perfect and exactly what we want it to be right away. Perhaps in the simple metaphor of gardening, we're reminded that faithfulness doesn't look like grandeur or flashy displays of religious fervor; it looks like simple, everyday obedience in the things God calls you to steward, starting at home.

I wonder how often we ask for God to provide but then wait for him to change our circumstances or to put us in an ideal situation before we're willing to use what he's already given us. Could it be that the abundance and provision God intends for you will come forth from the soil you're eagerly trying to uproot from?

I recently read these words from Scott Hubbard, editor at Desiring God, and it was a powerful reminder to me:

The story of Scripture is, in some ways, a story of *going.* . . . In creation, God intended Adam and Eve to fill not just Eden but the whole earth (Genesis 1:27–28). In redemption, God spreads his kingdom as Abraham goes from Ur (Genesis 12:1–3), Israel from Egypt (Exodus 3:10–12), the apostles from Jerusalem (Matthew 28:18–20), Paul and Barnabas from Antioch (Acts 13:1–3).

Yet alongside these memorable *goings* are less memorable, but still crucial, *stayings*. . . .

We live where we live, ultimately, because God has sent us here, at least for today. And the providential hand of God never moves without purpose.[1]

Hubbard went on to quote the Puritan author Samuel Rutherford, who once spoke of God as the gardener and himself as a plant:

The great Master-gardener, the Father of our Lord Jesus Christ, in a wonderful providence, with his own hand . . . planted me here, where, by his grace, in this part of his Vineyard, I grow. . . . And here I will abide, till the great Master of the Vineyard think fit to transplant me.[2]

Gardening is one part labor of our hands and one part God's sovereign care through creation. It's a reminder to us that God often chooses to provide at the intersection of our *just get started* and his *watch me do this.*

Maybe you've been waiting for someday or the perfect conditions to truly establish yourself in the place God has put you. Perhaps you're called to build a ministry but haven't yet because you're waiting for just the right people, partners, or resources. Our family felt the same way at times, but we learned to step out in faith and obedience even when we didn't have a perfect plan.

Could you begin today with small steps toward creating the infrastructure for that ministry? Or maybe you've known your own kind of displacement in your location and vocation, and God is now calling you to be at home with where you are? However you may be led to build houses, plant gardens, marry, and have children in your right-now seasons, know that doing so is a decision to abide and remain.

2. Seek the Peace and Prosperity of the City

I think the instruction to "seek the peace and prosperity of the city" in Jeremiah 29:7 (NIV) is, perhaps, the most convicting for me. Up until this point, God's instructions through Jeremiah were understandable and self-benefiting in a foreign land: Take care of yourself. Take care of your people. But now, God told his people to do what might seem nonintuitive: Do good in Babylon. Seek its good.

Wait, what?

God, don't you know these people worship other gods? Don't you know they're the cause of our misery? How can we seek their good and their peace when that's not their goal for us?

But Jeremiah spelled it out very clearly for them: "Also, seek the peace and prosperity of the city to which I have carried you into exile. Pray to the LORD for it, because if it prospers, you too will prosper" (v. 7 NIV). They were not to just settle in and make a life for themselves in a foreign land; they were to settle down and bring peace and good to their new hometown, to seek its good the way they'd seek their own. For the duration of their time there . . . which turned out to be a lot longer than they hoped.

This wasn't a call to simply endure, to grit your teeth and stick it out. These weren't instructions to get what you can and get out. This was a call to live and love right where they were, in obedience to the God who had allowed them to be sent there in the first place. I imagine, for the exiles, seeking the peace and prosperity of the city God placed them in included befriending, loving, and serving people who didn't love their God, who didn't honor the things they cared deeply about, and who lived contrary to the ways of God.

Can you think of someone or a whole bunch of someones who are difficult to love in your community? Who think differently than you? Who come from a background or worldview that feels foreign to you? I certainly can. God calls us to befriend them, love them, and serve them. But I think there's an even further exhortation here for us today. When we seek the peace and welfare of our town, city, or community, we prioritize our neighbors' dignity, well-being, and opportunity to flourish because we've been sent and supplied with the peace and abundance of hope in God.

This might look something like getting more involved in serving your community rather than withdrawing. It requires us to be part of the solution rather than just calling out the problems we see. Seeking peace and prosperity will look different for each of us as we consider where God has placed us, but the principle is the same: God may call us to put down roots and invest in the most unlikely of places to call home, but he will do so because when God's people choose to live surrendered lives where God calls them, they become conduits of peace, hope, change, and growth.

For us, this is a call to live and love as if our right now is what we really want (even if it isn't), in obedience to the God who has placed us right where we are. Do we pretend? Do we just fake it till we make it? No need to play the part; that's not the point. Instead, it's about letting our actions follow God's promises instead of our own understanding. I think it looks something akin to living into our identities in Christ, even if we don't fully feel like we're forgiven and free. We choose to take God at his word and respond with trust and obedience . . . because God is at work more than we know.

So what do we do when we feel far from home? Perhaps it's hard for you to be present in the season you're in when you're dreaming about a different one that might feel more like home. Or maybe, like me, you've been transplanted to a new city, new community, or new ministry and are starting over with relationships. Perhaps you still feel a bit like an outsider. Maybe you're physically not quite at home in the city where God has planted you. Perhaps you are an empty nester, and your home no longer feels or sounds like it once did. You spent so many years attending to the needs of your family that you've forgotten who God made you to be. You're wondering where you fit in service to the Lord now that the all-encompassing work of running your home has shifted.

Yet maybe it's not a season or location that doesn't feel like home for you today, but rather the trials the Lord has allowed in your life. Perhaps there's chronic pain, unexpected illness, a deep wound, or family conflict that feels like exile.

The charge to the Israelites and their call to faithfulness and fruitfulness began with simple things like home, family, and prayer. It didn't require prominent leadership positions in the community, stout bank accounts, Pinterest-worthy decor, or even that they feel settled in their new homes. It simply required that they be settled in the fact that God was their provision, their leader, their future, and their only defense.

Even as exiles, even as those who don't feel at home, God's people can build and bring the good news to the place where God has called them to be.

> This is what the LORD says: "When seventy years are completed for Babylon, I will come to you and fulfill my good promise to bring you back to this place. For I know the plans I have for you," declares the LORD, "plans to prosper you and not to harm you, plans to give you hope and a future. Then you will call on me and come and pray to me, and I will listen to you. You will seek me and find me when you seek me with all your heart. I will be found by you," declares the LORD, "and will bring you back from captivity. I will gather you from all the nations and places where I have banished you," declares the LORD, "and will bring you back to the place from which I carried you into exile." (Jeremiah 29:10–14 NIV)

This familiar ending to the prophet Jeremiah's words to God's people is not as much about our futures and good things to come as it is about God and his unshakable plans. Even if we are placed where we don't want to be, he is a God who carries us, who listens to us, who is knowable and intimate, and who will fulfill his promises. All we need to do is press in and take the first small step.

Just Start, Even If Poorly

Taking the first small step isn't always easy. If you get to know me, you'll find that I tend to get overwhelmed by all that's before me and either feel paralyzed with inaction because I don't know where to start or just give up because, if I can't do it well, I won't do it at all (yep, I was referring to myself earlier).

This is especially true when it comes to exercise. An exercise routine doesn't come naturally to me, so it's not uncommon for me to get overwhelmed at the idea of not being where I want to be with my health goals. I'll say things like, "Why can't I run an hour without dying?" And Troy will always say, "Just start where you are. Start with one small thing."

> If it's something worthy of doing well, it's something worthy of starting now, even if you're not good at it.

G. K. Chesterton once wrote a most freeing and convicting insight: "If a thing is worth doing, it is worth doing badly."[3] In other words, if it's something worthy of doing well, it's something worthy of starting now, even if you're not good at it.

When I feel behind in my Bible reading.
When I'm not yet an expert.
When I don't pray like I should.
When I haven't exercised or taken care of my body.
When I'm not the mom I want to be.

When I don't feel good at making friends.
When I don't love others like I should.

Just start where you are. Just start with one small thing, one small change. Anything worth doing is worth doing badly . . . for now.

Sometimes we underestimate the power of starting small and starting now.

So here's my question for both of us: What would you start doing today in obedience if you weren't afraid of failure, if you didn't worry about the future, and if you knew that God has you right where you are for a reason? What would you begin today?

Now, go do it.

Persevere

"What happens, though, once I start? How do I keep moving?" you might be asking. Let's think about it in terms of travel. It's amazing how much distance you can travel when you focus only on the very next step. Not the end goal, not the last stretch as you're about to arrive at the finish line. I'm talking about the step that comes after the one you just took. And then the next one. And then the next one. As it turns out, you make it to your destination by choosing to keep going.

As I'm writing to you in 2023, my oldest son just graduated from college and is now getting ready to move away for graduate school. Someday arrived sooner than I expected.

Later this year, my company, GraceLaced Co., will celebrate

ten years. I can hardly believe it. The someday I couldn't imagine on day one is somehow now a reality.

This summer, Troy and I will celebrate twenty-five years of marriage, by God's grace. What felt impossible two decades ago now eclipses any part of my life that existed before two unlikely sinners became one in Christ. That someday that once felt so far away is now a reminder that our days are passing quickly.

In a few months, I'll be entering the last two years of my forties. I feel like I'm only getting better with age. Someday wasn't so far away after all.

Friend, consider this a heartfelt reminder that, whatever you're navigating today, someday isn't as far away as you may think. We can choose to be on hold until we feel good about our life trajectories, or we can start where we are. The difference between biding your time with skepticism and taking steps of obedience right now is the person you become while you choose to persevere.

I want you to know that I haven't always chosen to really show up for the life God's given me, which is why this message matters so much to me. Even now, I still have to choose to remember the very truths of God's purposes I've unfolded in this book. As we've said before, the work of pressing in will not just naturally happen. You will not put down this book and magically operate from a continual place of joy, confidence, and hope in the places that apathy, fear, and lack of vision once occupied. (Wouldn't it be convenient if that were true?) No, you and I will have to fight for it. We will have to guard against coasting and growing complacent. We will have to explore, dig in, and be sure we fully grasp the mercies of God's grace through Christ.

I like Eugene Peterson's paraphrase of Philippians 2:12–13 in *The Message*:

> What I'm getting at, friends, is that you should simply keep on doing what you've done from the beginning. When I was living among you, you lived in responsive obedience. Now that I'm separated from you, keep it up. Better yet, redouble your efforts. Be energetic in your life of salvation, reverent and sensitive before God. That energy is *God's* energy, an energy deep within you, God himself willing and working at what will give him the most pleasure.

One thing is clear: Paul was telling the Philippians to persevere, to remain steadfast, and to keep pressing on in their efforts to walk with God, knowing that God is faithful.

Why would we think we can meet our days any differently?

The *both/and* exhortation to live fully dependent on God's sovereign care while fully engaged in the very next step we choose to take is a call to *both* faith *and* fortitude. That's not always easy to do. But it is necessary if we are going to fight to keep showing up.

George Müller, who was arguably one of the most effective evangelists of the nineteenth century, once said,

> This is one of the great secrets in connexion [*sic*] with successful service of the Lord; to work as if everything depended upon our diligence, and yet not to rest in the least upon our *exertions*, but upon the blessing of the Lord, who *alone* can cause your efforts to be made effectual, to the benefit of your fellow men or fellow believers.[4]

I love John Piper's response to Müller's secret for success:

> In other words, labor with all your might, but do not trust in
> your labor—trust in God. Plan hard, but don't trust in your
> plans— trust in God. Speak clearly and creatively, but don't
> trust in your speaking—trust in God. Sing, but don't trust
> in your singing—trust in God. Create and produce and lead
> and manage, but don't trust in your creativity and leadership
> and management and productivity—trust in God.[5]

You and I have been given good work to do, and sometimes it's going to feel like we're succeeding, while sometimes we'll be tempted to think we're failing miserably. What I want us to remember is that God is confident in accomplishing what he intends in our lives—"He who began a good work in you will bring it to completion at the day of Jesus Christ" (Philippians 1:6)—so don't worry about that! But he gives us an opportunity to gain the benefits of perseverance and . . .

> Consider it pure joy, my brothers and sisters, whenever you
> face trials of many kinds, because you know that the testing
> of your faith produces perseverance. Let perseverance finish
> its work so that you may be mature and complete, not lack-
> ing anything. (James 1:2–4 NIV)

As I remember this familiar passage of Scripture, I can't help but smile at how this sums up my whole heart for this now-and-not-yet message. I want us to be mature, complete, and lacking nothing, friend. *Yes, please.*

I want for you and me, both, to know the incomparable gift

of persevering *with* Christ, *through* Christ, *to* a destination— our forever someday with him. We're just passing through this earthly home, but, boy, is God shaping and molding us as we go.

It's a tall order to consider all our unwanted seasons and circumstances "pure joy," but we're one step closer to such a paradigm shift whenever we look at our right nows through the lens of God's Word . . . and press in.

Therefore

The New Testament writers tended to close their encouragement and reminders to fellow believers in the early church with a framework for persevering in faith: believe what Jesus said about himself and those who are in Christ and then respond accordingly. That's why we find the word *therefore* repeatedly throughout the letters to the churches. In light of the truth of who God is and what he's done, we *therefore* can and will live differently going forward. The call to action always follows the call to believe.

One of my favorite "therefores" is at the start of Hebrews 12:

Therefore, since we are surrounded by so great a cloud of witnesses, let us throw off everything that hinders and sin that so easily entangles. And let us run with perseverance the race marked out for us, fixing our eyes on Jesus, the pioneer and perfecter of faith. For the joy set before him he endured the cross, scorning its shame, and sat down at the right hand of the throne of God. (vv. 1–2 NIV)

Throw off entangling sin.

Run with perseverance.

Fix your eyes on Jesus.

Because Jesus is better than anything we could otherwise secure this side of heaven, we can live on purpose as we follow him to all that he has before us. And when the "therefore" of all that we believe of God's purposes compels us to simply take the next right step in perseverance, we start living hope-filled lives in our now, while our eyes are on all that is not yet.

So let this be the "therefore" call for us to persevere in our now-and-not-yet lives. Let all that we've seen in God's Word about our deserts, our nonblooming seasons, our hidden years, our not-yet-wonderful stories compel us to live courageously by faith today.

Oh, that you and I might do the improbable, face the impossible, withstand the intolerable, declare the inexpressible, and point the way to our Savior's transforming purposes when we—those who know the best is yet to come—choose to press in . . . right where we are.

TRUTH TO PRESS INTO

Where you find yourself tomorrow starts with what you choose today.

A LITURGY FOR WHEN YOU DON'T
KNOW WHAT TO DO

Here I stand, with the details of my past,
the not yets of my present,
and the unknowns of the future you hold.
I'm ready to be shaped and molded by my Maker,
that I might be an instrument of hope,
a vessel of truth, a conduit of grace.
May I not be content merely to believe—
to bask in the redemption that has been
purchased for me—without consequence or action.
But let me, instead, run the race set before me today,
with the finished work of Christ in view.
Consume me with the desire to run well.
Fuel me with the grace that ignites,
striving with all my might,
but only in all your strength, O Lord.
Persevering with joy,
because you hold me fast,
let me not grow weary in doing good.
I renounce my vain attempts at building
my own kingdom and remember, instead,
that I was made for yours.
Make me a builder, O Lord.
Make me a home for gospel hope—
no matter the duration or design.
I choose to begin today.
Help me begin today.
Amen.

Conclusion

I was praying over you this morning as our journey together comes to a close. I'm asking myself some questions: *Have I shared all that I wanted to share? Did I give the most real pieces of my heart that I can give here on these pages? Have I accomplished my goal of spurring you on in your specific not-yet place and season of life? Do you have a greater, more awe-inspiring view of God's faithfulness in motion, actively at work to accomplish his purposes in your life right now?*

I trust that he has and will continue to do what is needed in both your life and mine. But if I had one prayer for both of us, it would be that we would not get stuck, wishing we were somewhere else with a whole different set of circumstances, and miss what God is doing right now . . . even if our ideal, our dreams, our happy endings, our somedays feel so far away.

So this is me, leaning in to tell you:

You're not alone. You will make it.

This moment matters, and our God doesn't waste a thing.

Therefore, stay awake, stay present, and press in!

Conclusion

Run to *Jesus, not the other way.*

Get going and make the most of every opportunity!

Don't sit this season out.

Friend, if *carpe diem* literally means to "pluck the day (when it is ripe)," then we—who believe that being with Christ face-to-face and being conformed into his likeness is the fruit of harvest we ultimately long for—can seize the day, *today*, in the light of what God will produce in his time.

And maybe this is even more accurate: *carpe diem in luce aeternitatis*—literally "seize the day in light of eternity" in Latin. It's our clarion call to look forward to someday while we stay faithful right now. Eye on the prize with our hand to the plow. Remember the words of Paul: "But one thing I do: forgetting what lies behind and straining forward to what lies ahead, I press on toward the goal for the prize of the upward call of God in Christ Jesus" (Philippians 3:13–14).

Seize the day in light of eternity.

So press on, friend. Lean in. There's no time to stay stuck in the past or to be on the fence about today. You've been given hard and wonderful tasks only you are gifted enough to do. You're not right where you are on accident.

This is not a passive, wait-and-see game plan, friend; it is a hand-to-the-plow-and-trust-God way of life. And he—our God who is faithful yesterday, today, and forever—will complete what he has begun in us. He promised to.

> Now to him who is able to keep you from stumbling and to present you blameless before the presence of his glory with great joy, to the only God, our Savior, through Jesus Christ

our Lord, be glory, majesty, dominion, and authority, before
all time and now and forever. Amen. (Jude vv. 24–25)

Are you in?

Start where you are and press in, friend, because God has
been and will always be faithful in our now and not yet.

I love you; Christ loves you more.

XO,
RCS

A LITURGY FOR NOW AND NOT YET

You, O God, are . . .
the Lord of my wrestlings,
the King of my yearnings,
the Creator of my giftings,
the Rescuer of my wanderings,
the Sustainer of my insufficiencies,
the Provider for my impossibilities,
the Deliverer for my insurmountable,
the Way in my wanderings,
the Alpha of my beginnings,
the Omega of my endings,
and the Keeper of all that is yet to come.
Praise you, O God, for all that is yet to come.
Amen.

The Theological Framework of the Now and Not Yet

There's a deeper theological concept undergirding the themes we've looked at in this book. It's what biblical scholars have called the "already, but not yet," or the "now and not yet" framework.

This biblical perspective deeply impacted my walk with Christ years ago when I first encountered it and continues to impact the way I understand and respond to God's Word today. We didn't have the space to fully get into that theology in this book, so, for those of you seeking to dig a little deeper, I want to take some time now to sum it up here and encourage you to further study this biblical lens as you look to God's Word and consider yourself within the realities of this present age and the unfolding of the age to come.

The lens through which the New Testament writers encouraged believers is one that looks both to what Christ has already done in this present age and what he is yet to do in the age to come. The first coming of Christ—his life, death, and resurrection—marked the beginning of redemptive history, as the gift of salvation was made possible to all who believe. The second coming of Christ is Jesus' glorious and physical return to judge the earth at the end of the age, accompanied by the resurrection of the dead. This second coming, or second advent, inaugurates the eternal rule and reign of Christ in the forever kingdom of God.

The age between his first and second comings is what the Bible calls "the last days" (Hebrews 1:2) and is the age we live in now, one where the promises of God's redemption story are already true but are yet to be fully revealed or experienced completely. The tension of this in-between age is the context for all that we've discussed in this book; this is the theological tension of living in light of what has already been accomplished for us in Christ and also what has yet to be fully realized when he comes again. We see this play out in the realities of our Christian life.

When we trust in Jesus, we are *already* forgiven, *already* made right, *already* recipients of the riches of God's grace, *already* given a new identity, *already* fully loved, *already* called sons and daughters.

We are transferred from darkness into light. But we have yet to fully experience that transformation. And there are other not yets to our redemption stories:

- We're already forgiven of our sin, but we are *not yet free from sin.*
- We're already given new identities in Christ, but we are *not yet fully formed as a new creation.*
- We're already now citizens of heaven, but we are *not yet home with our God.*

This not-yet age is not the end of the story. The theological framework through which we can understand our present age ultimately sees all the promises of God's faithfulness come to fruition in our heavenly home when we are fully made new, fully at home, fully free of sin:

> And I heard a loud voice from the throne saying, "Behold, the dwelling place of God is with man. He will dwell with them, and they will be his people, and God himself will be with them as their God. He will wipe away every tear from their eyes, and death shall be no more, neither shall there be mourning, nor crying, nor pain anymore, for the former things have passed away." (Revelation 21:3–4)

Because the true hope of Christ's return, and thus the not yet, is sure, we can live in light of all that is already ours in Christ. After all, this is not our home; we are but pilgrims passing through this not-yet world. If we let the already of our redemption in Christ fuel our joy and hope today, the yet-to-be-completed promises of Christ's return and eternal victory will free us to walk in grace moment by moment with our eyes on the day when our transformation, and God's eternal rule and reign, are entirely fulfilled.

My hope, dear believer, is that this basic and simple summary might spark further study of this theological framework. The goal of digging deeper into any theology is to help us grow in our understanding of God and his ways, that we might love him, know him, and walk more closely with him. May the wonder of God's faithfulness in coming to save sinners like you and me the first time, and his promise to come again to make all things new and right forevermore, spur us on in faithfulness today.

There is a glorious dwelling place provided by Jesus Christ for all His believing people. The world that now is, is not their rest: they are pilgrims and strangers in it. Heaven is their home.

J. C. Ryle, *Heaven*

Five Steps to Help You Flip the Script About Your Hard Season

Change the narratives you're rehearsing right now and press into trusting God for what's not yet by considering your current hard season through five steps that help you flip the script:

1. **Praise God for who he is.** Remind yourself who God says he is in the Bible. Begin with God's character and his ways. Declare the truths about who God is and why that matters in your circumstance. Here are some scriptures that can help you get started:
   - He is Creator: Genesis 1:1–25.
   - He is the Good Shepherd: Psalm 23; John 10:14–18.
   - He is Light of the World: John 9:5; 1 John 1:5; Psalm 18:28.
   - He is love: 1 John 4:16; Romans 5:8.
   - He is our salvation: Isaiah 12:2–6; 1 John 4:14.

2. **Agree with God about who he says you are.** First identify, then believe what God says is true about who you are in Christ. What about your identity in him speaks to your current situation?

3. **Remember what God has done.** Tell yourself of God's faithfulness in the past from what you read in his Word and what you've personally experienced.

4. **Choose one small step of obedience.** Take inventory of the opportunities God has given you—whether you like them or not. If you believe that he is sovereign and good, what can you take a step of faith in today?

5. **Share your hard season with your community.** We're not meant to walk through our hard seasons in isolation. When we practice declaring truth to one another, for one another, and over one another, we remember that we're not alone.

Are you ready to give it a try? Here are a few examples to get you started, along with room for you to practice flipping the script on your own narratives:

My narrative: If I disappoint someone or don't perform to standard, the people I care about will leave me and abandon me.

Flip the script: God's Word says he will never leave me or forsake me. Even though I feel forgotten, I can trust that he is with me in the midst of this desert season.

My narrative: I'm never going to be good enough to get anywhere with my goals and dreams.

Flip the script: In Christ, I have been equipped with everything I need for life and godliness. Even though I feel woefully inadequate, I will trust that his power is enough.

My narrative: I can only trust myself; everyone else will hurt or fail me.

Flip the script: I have tasted and seen God's provision over and over. Even though this season has brought so much heartbreak, I know he will provide for me and my family.

My narrative: I don't have any close friends, and there aren't many opportunities to meet new people.

Flip the script: God has put me in a neighborhood and given me relationships with my neighbors. Even though they may not be the friends I'd choose because we don't have much in common, I can invest in the people God has put me in proximity to.

Your Turn

My narrative:

Flip the script:

My narrative:

Flip the script:

My narrative:

Flip the script:

My narrative:

Flip the script:

Start Where You Are
Self-Assessment

Starting where you are can feel like a vague, faraway concept, making it hard to know how to, well, start. If you're feeling confused and unsure of what to do, here's a quick self-assessment you can use to help direct your next steps.

Think about a life circumstance that feels "far from home" to you right now. Then, using the framework of God's instructions to his people through Jeremiah 29:4–14, assess your current context:

1. How is God calling you to build infrastructure for what he's given you or called you to?
2. In what way(s) can you cultivate growth with what you already have?
3. Who are the people God has placed around you, and

how can you leave a legacy with those already in your spheres of influence?

4. How can you seek not just your own wellness but peace and good in your context, or in your community?

Scriptures

1. When Right Now Isn't What You Want

. . . and the LORD drove the sea back by a strong east wind all night and made the sea dry land, and the waters were divided. And the people of Israel went into the midst of the sea on dry ground, the waters being a wall to them on their right hand and on their left. (Exodus 14:21–22)

This is what the LORD says—
        he who made a way through the sea,
        a path through the mighty waters,
  who drew out the chariots and horses,
        the army and reinforcements together,
  and they lay there, never to rise again,
        extinguished, snuffed out like
  a wick:

"Forget the former things;
    do not dwell on the past.
See, I am doing a new thing!
    Now it springs up; do you not
perceive it?
I am making a way in the wilderness
    and streams in the wasteland."
(Isaiah 43:16–19 NIV)

This is the day that the LORD has made;
    let us rejoice and be glad in it.
(Psalm 118:24)

2. Restlessness as an Invitation

Now the serpent was more crafty than any of the wild animals the LORD God had made. He said to the woman, "Did God really say, 'You must not eat from any tree in the garden'?"

The woman said to the serpent, "We may eat fruit from the trees in the garden, but God did say, 'You must not eat fruit from the tree that is in the middle of the garden, and you must not touch it, or you will die.'"

"You will not certainly die," the serpent said to the woman. "For God knows that when you eat from it your eyes will be opened, and you will be like God, knowing good and evil."

When the woman saw that the fruit of the tree was

good for food and pleasing to the eye, and also desirable for gaining wisdom, she took some and ate it. She also gave some to her husband, who was with her, and he ate it. Then the eyes of both of them were opened, and they realized they were naked; so they sewed fig leaves together and made coverings for themselves. (Genesis 3:1–7 NIV)

Come to me, all who labor and are heavy laden, and I will give you rest. Take my yoke upon you, and learn from me, for I am gentle and lowly in heart, and you will find rest for your souls. For my yoke is easy, and my burden is light. (Matthew 11:28–30)

Be still, and know that I am God.
(Psalm 46:10)

3. Hidden Doesn't Mean Forgotten

Many Samaritans from that town believed in him because of the woman's testimony. (John 4:39)

4. You Don't Have to Be Blooming to Be Growing

Do not be deceived: God is not mocked, for whatever one sows, that will he also reap. For the one who sows to his own flesh will from the flesh reap corruption, but the one who sows to the Spirit will from the Spirit reap eternal life. And let us not grow weary of doing good, for in due season we will reap, if we do not give up. (Galatians 6:7–9)

As for you, you meant evil against me, but God meant it for good, to bring it about that many people should be kept alive, as they are today. (Genesis 50:20)

> Blessed is the one
>> who does not walk in step with the
> wicked
> or stand in the way that sinners take
>> or sit in the company of mockers,
> but whose delight is in the law of the LORD,
>> and who meditates on his law day
> and night.
> That person is like a tree planted by streams
> of water,
>> which yields its fruit in season
> and whose leaf does not wither—
>> whatever they do prospers.
>> (Psalm 1:1–3 NIV)

Let us draw near with a true heart in full assurance of faith, with our hearts sprinkled clean from an evil conscience and our bodies washed with pure water. Let us hold fast the confession of our hope without wavering, for he who promised is faithful. (Hebrews 10:22–23)

5. Someday Is Made Up of Thousands of Right Nows

A disciple is not above his teacher, but everyone when he is fully trained will be like his teacher. (Luke 6:40)

I have fought the good fight, I have finished the race, I have kept the faith. Now there is in store for me the crown of righteousness, which the Lord, the righteous Judge, will award to me on that day—and not only to me, but also to all who have longed for his appearing. (2 Timothy 4:7–8 NIV)

Do you not know that in a race all the runners run, but only one receives the prize? So run that you may obtain it. Every athlete exercises self-control in all things. They do it to receive a perishable wreath, but we an imperishable. So I do not run aimlessly; I do not box as one beating the air. But I discipline my body and keep it under control, lest after preaching to others I myself should be disqualified. (1 Corinthians 9:24–27)

We destroy arguments and every lofty opinion raised against the knowledge of God, and take every thought captive to obey Christ. (2 Corinthians 10:5)

So you also must consider yourselves dead to sin and alive to God in Christ Jesus. (Romans 6:11)

And above all these put on love, which binds everything together in perfect harmony. (Colossians 3:14)

Therefore, if anyone is in Christ, he is a new creation. The old has passed away; behold, the new has come. (2 Corinthians 5:17)

Do not be conformed to this world, but be transformed by the renewal of your mind, that by testing you may discern what is the will of God, what is good and acceptable and perfect. (Romans 12:2)

But be doers of the word, and not hearers only, deceiving yourselves. For if anyone is a hearer of the word and not a doer, he is like a man who looks intently at his natural face in a mirror. For he looks at himself and goes away and at once forgets what he was like. But the one who looks into the perfect law, the law of liberty, and perseveres, being no hearer who forgets but a doer who acts, he will be blessed in his doing. (James 1:22–25)

6. Chaos Produces Character

And we know that in all things God works for the good of those who love him, who have been called according to his purpose. (Romans 8:28 NIV)

Who has cleft a channel for the torrents of
   rain
         and a way for the thunderbolt,
   to bring rain on a land where no man is,
         on the desert in which there is
   no man,
   to satisfy the waste and desolate land,
         and to make the ground sprout with
         grass? (Job 38:25–27)

And God made the two great lights—the greater light to
rule the day and the lesser light to rule the night—and
the stars. And God set them in the expanse of the heav-
ens to give light on the earth, to rule over the day and
over the night, and to separate the light from the darkness. And God saw that it was good. (Genesis 1:16–18)

But concerning the day and hour no one knows, not
even the angels of heaven, nor the Son, but the Father
only. (Matthew 24:36)

And he is before all things, and in him all things hold
together. (Colossians 1:17)

For all the promises of God find their Yes in him. That
is why it is through him that we utter our Amen to
God for his glory. (2 Corinthians 1:20)

And he who was seated on the throne said, "Behold, I
am making all things new." (Revelation 21:5)

Do not think I have come to abolish the Law or the Prophets; I have not come to abolish them but to fulfill them. (Matthew 5:17)

7. God's Callings Are His Enablings

And we know that for those who love God all things work together for good, for those who are called according to his purpose. (Romans 8:28)

Now to him who is able to do far more abundantly than all that we ask or think, according to the power at work within us . . . (Ephesians 3:20)

And I am sure of this, that he who began a good work in you will bring it to completion at the day of Jesus Christ. (Philippians 1:6)

> I lift up my eyes to the hills.
>> From where does my help come?
> My help comes from the LORD,
>> who made heaven and earth.
> (Psalm 121:1–2)

Behold, the Lamb of God, who takes away the sin of the world! This is he of whom I said, "After me comes a man who ranks before me, because he was before me." (John 1:29–30)

Scriptures

Therefore, since we are surrounded by so great a cloud of witnesses, let us also lay aside every weight, and sin which clings so closely, and let us run with endurance the race that is set before us, looking to Jesus, the founder and perfecter of our faith, who for the joy that was set before him endured the cross, despising the shame, and is seated at the right hand of the throne of God. (Hebrews 12:1–2)

And we all, with unveiled face, beholding the glory of the Lord, are being transformed into the same image from one degree of glory to another. (2 Corinthians 3:18)

But he said to me, "My grace is sufficient for you, for my power is made perfect in weakness." Therefore I will boast all the more gladly of my weaknesses, so that the power of Christ may rest upon me. For the sake of Christ, then, I am content with weaknesses, insults, hardships, persecutions, and calamities. For when I am weak, then I am strong. (2 Corinthians 12:9–10)

He said, "Take your son, your only son Isaac, whom you love, and go to the land of Moriah, and offer him there as a burnt offering on one of the mountains of which I shall tell you." (Genesis 22:2)

And Isaac said to his father Abraham, "My father!" And he said, "Here I am, my son." He said, "Behold, the fire and the wood, but where is the lamb for a burnt offering?" Abraham said, "God will provide

for himself the lamb for a burnt offering, my son."
(Genesis 22:7–8)

He said, "Do not lay your hand on the boy or do anything to him, for now I know that you fear God, seeing
you have not withheld your son, your only son, from
me." And Abraham lifted up his eyes and looked, and
behold, behind him was a ram, caught in a thicket by his
horns. And Abraham went and took the ram and offered
it up as a burnt offering instead of his son. So Abraham
called the name of that place, "The LORD will provide";
as it is said to this day, "On the mount of the LORD it
shall be provided." (Genesis 22:12–14)

8. When It's Not
Just a Season

O God, you are my God; earnestly I seek you;
    my soul thirsts for you;
my flesh faints for you,
    as in a dry and weary land where
there is no water.
(Psalm 63:1)

I will take you to be my people, and I will be your God,
and you shall know that I am the LORD your God,
who has brought you out from under the burdens of the
Egyptians. (Exodus 6:7)

And he humbled you and let you hunger and fed you with manna, which you did not know, nor did your fathers know, that he might make you know that man does not live by bread alone, but man lives by every word that comes from the mouth of the LORD. (Deuteronomy 8:3)

Take care lest you forget the LORD your God. (Deuteronomy 8:11)

Beware lest you say in your heart, "My power and the might of my hand have gotten me this wealth." (Deuteronomy 8:17)

> O God, you are my God; earnestly I seek you;
>> my soul thirsts for you;
> my flesh faints for you,
>> as in a dry and weary land where
> there is no water.
> So I have looked upon you in the sanctuary,
>> beholding your power and glory.
> Because your steadfast love is better than life,
>> my lips will praise you.
> So I will bless you as long as I live;
>> in your name I will lift up my hands.
> My soul will be satisfied as with fat and
> rich food,
>> and my mouth will praise you with
> joyful lips,

when I remember you upon my bed,
    and meditate on you in the watches
of the night;
for you have been my help,
    and in the shadow of your wings I
will sing for joy.
My soul clings to you;
    your right hand upholds me.
(Psalm 63:1–8)

9. The Stories
We Tell Ourselves

Turn to me and be gracious to me,
    for I am lonely and afflicted.
(Psalm 25:16)

In the day of my trouble I seek the Lord;
    in the night my hand is stretched
out without wearying;
    my soul refuses to be comforted.
(Psalm 77:2)

I will ponder all your work,
    and meditate on your mighty deeds.
Your way, O God, is holy.
    What god is great like our God?
(Psalm 77:12–13)

Your way was through the sea,
>your path through the great waters;
>yet your footprints were unseen.
You led your people like a flock
>by the hand of Moses and Aaron.
(Psalm 77:19–20)

We are afflicted in every way, but not crushed; perplexed, but not driven to despair; persecuted, but not forsaken; struck down, but not destroyed. (2 Corinthians 4:8–9)

So we do not lose heart. Though our outer self is wasting away, our inner self is being renewed day by day. For this light momentary affliction is preparing for us an eternal weight of glory beyond all comparison, as we look not to the things that are seen but to the things that are unseen. For the things that are seen are transient, but the things that are unseen are eternal. (2 Corinthians 4:16–18)

In this you rejoice, though now for a little while, if necessary, you have been grieved by various trials, so that the tested genuineness of your faith—more precious than gold that perishes though it is tested by fire—may be found to result in praise and glory and honor at the revelation of Jesus Christ. (1 Peter 1:6–7)

Blessed be the God and Father of our Lord Jesus Christ! According to his great mercy, he has caused us to be born again to a living hope through the resurrection of Jesus Christ from the dead, to an inheritance that is imperishable, undefiled, and unfading, kept in heaven for you, who by God's power are being guarded through faith for a salvation ready to be revealed in the last time. (1 Peter 1:3–5)

Not only that, but we rejoice in our sufferings, knowing that suffering produces endurance, and endurance produces character, and character produces hope, and hope does not put us to shame, because God's love has been poured into our hearts through the Holy Spirit who has been given to us. (Romans 5:3–5)

10. Start Where You Are

This is what the LORD Almighty, the God of Israel, says to all those I carried into exile from Jerusalem to Babylon: "Build houses and settle down; plant gardens and eat what they produce. Marry and have sons and daughters; find wives for your sons and give your daughters in marriage, so that they too may have sons and daughters. Increase in number there; do not decrease. Also, seek the peace and prosperity of the city to which I have carried you into exile. Pray to the LORD for it, because if it prospers, you too will prosper." (Jeremiah 29:4–7 NIV)

Abide in me, as I in you. As the branch cannot bear fruit by itself, unless it abides in the vine, neither can you, unless you abide in me. I am the vine; you are the branches. Whoever abides in me and I in him, he it is that bears much fruit, for apart from me you can do nothing. (John 15:4–5)

Also, seek the peace and prosperity of the city to which I have carried you into exile. Pray to the LORD for it, because if it prospers, you too will prosper. (Jeremiah 29:7 NIV)

This is what the LORD says: "When seventy years are completed for Babylon, I will come to you and fulfill my good promise to bring you back to this place. For I know the plans I have for you," declares the LORD, "plans to prosper you and not to harm you, plans to give you hope and a future. Then you will call on me and come and pray to me, and I will listen to you. You will seek me and find me when you seek me with all your heart. I will be found by you," declares the LORD, "and will bring you back from captivity. I will gather you from all the nations and places where I have banished you," declares the LORD, "and will bring you back to the place from which I carried you into exile." (Jeremiah 29:10–14 NIV)

What I'm getting at, friends, is that you should simply keep on doing what you've done from the beginning. When I was living among you, you lived in responsive obedience. Now that I'm separated from you, keep it up. Better yet, redouble your efforts. Be energetic in your life of salvation, reverent and sensitive before God. That energy is *God's* energy, an energy deep within you, God himself willing and working at what will give him the most pleasure. (Philippians 2:12–13 THE MESSAGE)

He who began a good work in you will bring it to completion at the day of Jesus Christ. (Philippians 1:6)

Consider it pure joy, my brothers and sisters, whenever you face trials of many kinds, because you know that the testing of your faith produces perseverance. Let perseverance finish its work so that you may be mature and complete, not lacking anything. (James 1:2–4 NIV)

Therefore, since we are surrounded by so great a cloud of witnesses, let us throw off everything that hinders and the sin that so easily entangles. And let us run with perseverance the race marked out for us, fixing our eyes on Jesus, the pioneer and perfecter of faith. For the joy set before him he endured the cross, scorning its shame, and sat down at the right hand of the throne of God. (Hebrews 12:1–2 NIV)

Conclusion

But one thing I do: forgetting what lies behind and straining forward to what lies ahead, I press on toward the goal for the prize of the upward call of God in Christ Jesus. (Philippians 3:13–14)

Now to him who is able to keep you from stumbling and to present you blameless before the presence of his glory with great joy, to the only God, our Savior, through Jesus Christ our Lord, be glory, majesty, dominion, and authority, before all time and now and forever. Amen. (Jude vv. 24–25)

The Theological Framework of the Now and Not Yet

Long ago, at many times and in many ways, God spoke to our fathers by the prophets, but in these last days he has spoken to us by his Son, whom he appointed the heir of all things, through whom also he created the world. (Hebrews 1:1–2)

And I heard a loud voice from the throne saying, "Behold, the dwelling place of God is with man. He will dwell with them, and they will be his people, and God himself will be with them as their God. He will wipe away every tear from their eyes, and death shall be no more, neither shall there be mourning, nor crying, nor pain anymore, for the former things have passed away." (Revelation 21:3–4)

Acknowledgments

Much of this book was written while this very message was tested and tried in real time. It was a hard-won message, and I'm grateful to those who fought for me:

Troy, you tirelessly embody a now-and-not-yet perseverance. Thank you for teaching me how to press in, press on, and how to carpe diem in light of eternity.

Caleb, Liam, Judah, Stone, Asa, and Haddon: you love your mama so well; I couldn't do this without your encouragement.

Eve, you don't have to read every word, but you do. You don't have to care about these works as if they were your own, but you do. I'm so grateful for a friend like you.

GraceLaced Team (Ana-Lidia, Annalea, Camille, Eve, Jen, Mallory, and Rachael), you freed me up to do this work God's called me to, and you make creating beauty so fun, special, and truly significant. Thank you for being the dream team.

My agent, Jenni Burke, thank you for the care and consideration you give in championing my voice. I'm grateful for your friendship and guidance.

Acknowledgments

Jessica, thank you for being the best brainstorming, analyzing, relentlessly thoughtful editor I could hope for. Thank you for stewarding this message with me and carrying it with me to the finish line.

To my Nelson Books team—Andrew Stoddard, Jessica Wong Rogers, Brigitta Nortker, Kristen Golden, Lisa Beech, Claire Drake, Chris Sigfrids, Meg Schmidt, and Kristen Sasamoto— I'm so grateful for the way you cheer me on and bring excellence to every step of this book's journey.

And to my house-church family: You have encouraged, prayed, and built me up through the entirety of writing this book. I couldn't ask for a sweeter community to grow with. Thank you for being part of God's great provision in our now and not yet.

To my heavenly Father, who is so patient with me: You are worthy of praise for all that you've done and are yet to do. Thank you for giving me every reason to press in right now . . . even now.

Notes

Chapter 1: When Right Now Isn't What You Want

1. Elisabeth Elliot, *Keep a Quiet Heart: 100 Devotional Readings* (Grand Rapids: Revell, 2022), 20; emphasis in original.

Chapter 2: Restlessness as an Invitation

1. *Oxford Advanced Learner's Dictionary*, s.v. "restlessness," https://www .oxfordlearnersdictionaries.com/us/definition/english/restlessness.
2. Augustine, *The Confessions*, trans. Henry Chadwick (Oxford University Press, 2008), 1.1.1.

Chapter 3: Hidden Doesn't Mean Forgotten

1. David Mathis, "How God Became a Man: What Jesus Did for Thirty Years," Desiring God, December 8, 2016, https://www.desiringgod .org/articles/how-god-became-a-man.
2. Jon Bloom, "Joseph: Staying Faithful When Things Just Get Worse," Desiring God, March 1, 2010, https://www.desiringgod.org/articles /joseph-staying-faithful-when-things-just-get-worse.

Chapter 4: You Don't Have to Be Blooming to Be Growing

1. Paul David Tripp, *Instruments in the Redeemer's Hands: People in Need of Change Helping People in Need of Change* (Phillipsburg, NJ: P&R Publishing, 2002), 63.

Chapter 5: Someday Is Made Up of Thousands of Right Nows

1. Ruth Chou Simons, *When Strivings Cease: Replacing the Myth of Self-Improvement with the Good News of Life-Transforming Grace* (Nashville: Thomas Nelson, 2021).
2. "The journey is the thing" is a quote widely attributed to Homer but without textual support.
3. G. K. Chesterton, "How I Met the President," in *Tremendous Trifles* (1909; repr., Berkeley, CA: Mint Editions, 2021), 68.
4. Malcolm Gladwell, *Outliers: The Story of Success* (Boston: Little, Brown and Company, 2008), 39–42.
5. Angela Duckworth, *Grit: The Power of Passion and Perseverance* (New York: Scribner, 2016).
6. Jeffrey R. Young, "Researcher Behind '10,000-Hour Rule' Says Good Teaching Matters, Not Just Practice," EdSurge, May 5, 2020, https://www.edsurge.com/news/2020–05–05-researcher-behind-10–000-hour-rule-says-good-teaching-matters-not-just-practice.
7. Arnold Lobel, "Tomorrow," *Days with Frog and Toad* (New York: HarperCollins, 1979), 5.
8. Lobel, "Tomorrow," 9–10.
9. *Oxford Dictionary of Proverbs*, 6th ed. (Oxford University Press, 2015), s.v. "Never put off till tomorrow what you can do today," https://proverbs_new.en-academic.com/1932/never_put_off_till_tomorrow_what_you_can_do_today.

Chapter 6: Chaos Produces Character

1. "Aren't Sure? Brain Is Primed for Learning, " YaleNews, July 19, 2018, https://news.yale.edu/2018/07/19/arent-sure-brain-primed-learning.
2. "Aren't Sure? Brain Is Primed."
3. Jessica Stillman, "Science Has Just Confirmed That If You're Not Outside Your Comfort Zone You're Not Learning," Inc.com, August 14, 2018, https://www.inc.com/jessica-stillman/want-to-learn-faster-make-your-life-more-unpredictable.html.
4. Stillman, "Science Has Just Confirmed."
5. Stillman, "Science Has Just Confirmed."
6. Timothy Keller (@timkellernyc), "God will only give you what you would have asked for if you knew everything he knows," X, June 17, 2019, 1:09 p.m., https://twitter.com/timkellernyc/status/1140682773134544896?lang=en.

7. John Piper, "Use Means, but Trust in God," Desiring God, February 17, 2004, https://www.desiringgod.org/messages/use-means-but-trust-in-god.

Chapter 9: The Stories We Tell Ourselves
1. Paul David Tripp, *New Morning Mercies: A Daily Gospel Devotional* (Wheaton, IL: Crossway, 2014), February 4.
2. Ruth Chou Simons, *TruthFilled: The Practice of Preaching to Yourself through Every Season* (Nashville: Lifeway, 2020).
3. Dean Collins, "Why Your Spine Goes Out of Alignment?" Collins Chiropractic Health & Wellness Centre, June 20, 2022, https://drcollins.ca/spine-goes-out-of-alignment.

Chapter 10: Start Where You Are
1. Scott Hubbard, "Love the Place You Want to Leave," Desiring God, May 5, 2023, https://www.desiringgod.org/articles/love-the-place-you-want-to-leave.
2. Samuel Rutherford, *Letters of Samuel Rutherford: With a Sketch of His Life*, ed. Andrew Alexander Bonar (New York: Robert Carter & Brothers, 1863), 93.
3. G. K. Chesterton, "Folly and Female Education," *What's Wrong with the World* (1910; repr., San Francisco: Ignatius Press, 1994), chapter 41.
4. George Müller, as quoted in John Piper, "Use Means, but Trust in God," Desiring God, February 17, 2004; emphasis in original, https://www.desiringgod.org/messages/use-means-but-trust-in-god.
5. Piper, "Use Means, but Trust in God."

About the Author

Ruth Chou Simons is a *Wall Street Journal* bestselling and award-winning author of several books and Bible studies, including *GraceLaced*, *Beholding and Becoming*, *When Strivings Cease*, and *TruthFilled*. She is an artist, entrepreneur, podcaster, and speaker, using each of these platforms to sow the Word of God into people's hearts. Through social media and her online shoppe at GraceLaced.com, Simons shares her journey of God's grace intersecting daily life with word and art. Ruth and her husband, Troy, are grateful parents to six boys—their greatest adventure.

COMPANION BIBLE STUDY
FOR YOUR CHURCH AND SMALL GROUP

AVAILABLE WHEREVER BOOKS ARE SOLD.